CALM KIDS, HAPPY HEARTS

Dr Andrew Leech

First published 2024 by Andrew Leech

Produced by Independent Ink
independentink.com.au

Copyright © Andrew Leech 2024

The moral right of the author to be identified as the author of this work has been asserted.

All rights reserved. Except as permitted under the *Australian Copyright Act 1968*, no part of this publication may be reproduced, stored in a retrieval system, or transmitted in any form or by any means, electronic, mechanical, photocopying, recording or otherwise, without prior written permission from the publisher. All enquiries should be made to the author.

Cover design by Catucci Design
Edited by Brooke Lyons
Internal design by Independent Ink
Typeset in 11.5/17 pt Utopia Std by Post Pre-press Group, Brisbane
Cover image: Ljupco / iStock
Images on pages 11, 48, 71 and 163 were generated with the assistance of AI

ISBN 978-0-646-88344-1 (paperback)
ISBN 978-1-7636738-0-9 (epub)
ISBN 978-1-7636738-1-6 (kindle)

Disclaimer
The information provided in this book is intended for general informational purposes only. It is not intended to be a substitute for professional medical advice, diagnosis or treatment. The content within this book is based on research and general knowledge up to the time of publication (2024) and may not encompass all aspects of anxiety or individual circumstances.

Parents, educators, caregivers and readers are encouraged to use this book as a helpful resource to better understand anxiety in children. However, if you have concerns about a child's health, mental health or specific symptoms related to anxiety, it is crucial to seek guidance from a qualified medical or mental health professional. Each child's experience with anxiety is unique, and accurate assessment and appropriate interventions require individualised attention from trained professionals.

Therefore, the information presented in this book should not be considered a replacement for a comprehensive evaluation by a qualified healthcare provider. The author, publisher and contributors to this book are not liable for any actions taken based on the information presented herein. Always consult a qualified healthcare professional for specific advice or concerns about a child's health or wellbeing.

If you or anyone you know is feeling at risk of self-harm or suicide, it is crucial to seek immediate help and support. You can reach out to emergency services by dialling 000. Additionally, Lifeline Australia provides 24/7 crisis support and suicide prevention services at 13 11 14. Beyond Blue offers support for anxiety, depression and suicide prevention through its helpline at 1300 22 4636.

Remember, help is available, and reaching out can make a significant difference to someone's life.

Contents

Introduction	1
Part I: Understanding Anxiety	
What is Anxiety?	13
What Causes Anxiety?	28
What is an Anxiety Disorder?	42
Part II: Managing Anxiety	
Creating a Secure Base	69
Practical Ways to Help Your Child	81
Navigating Challenging Behaviours	106
Part III: Treating Anxiety	
Choosing a GP	135
Psychological Treatments	143
Treatment Plans	150
Medication	156
Case Studies	173
Conclusion	197
Resources	199
Acknowledgements	211
About the Author	213
References	217

Introduction

> *'Life brings inevitable challenges. Our job is to not protect children from the ups and downs that life throws, but to teach them that they are up to the challenge.'*
>
> — BEV AISBETT

Mental health problems in childhood can have a substantial impact on wellbeing. There is strong evidence that mental disorders in childhood and adolescence predict mental illness in adulthood.[1] At the same time, childhood presents the greatest opportunity for intervention. Investing in prevention and early intervention gives children the best opportunity for good mental health and wellbeing. For high-risk groups, such as children affected by violence, abuse, maltreatment or poverty, early intervention can help reduce disparities between the mental health of these children and children in psychologically healthy environments.[2]

There is no one-size-fits-all approach to understanding a child's emotions. Every child is special and unique, and they are influenced by both the world around them and their genetics. As a GP, I have learned it is this uniqueness that we need to allow time and space to explore. To support them we need to understand what goes into making that whole child.

Many of us have periods of anxiety, sometimes severe enough to stop us in our tracks. For children this might mean missing school, falling behind academically or struggling with regulating their emotions.

Children display emotions through their behaviour. They don't always have the words to express what it is that is making them anxious. This is particularly true for younger children, but even adolescents can exhibit behaviours that may seem confronting, such as self-harm. The self-harm is an action that represents pain and suffering internally along with an inability to know how to express the feeling or cause.

Some children become aggressive, hitting or screaming when they are anxious. This can be extremely difficult to handle. The behaviour, like the tip of an iceberg, represents emotions occurring below the surface (see figure 1). We need to find out what those emotions are to identify what is leading to those outbursts.

Children and teenagers who regularly exhibit behaviours such as these need help to express what is going on for them. They need help acknowledging that there is a deeper issue, which may well be an anxiety disorder.

Some children simply need time to process their emotions and may only experience these challenges in relation to a specific situation. We face many difficult periods in our lives and children and teenagers are not exempt from this. Something that might

FIGURE 1: THE ANXIETY ICEBERG

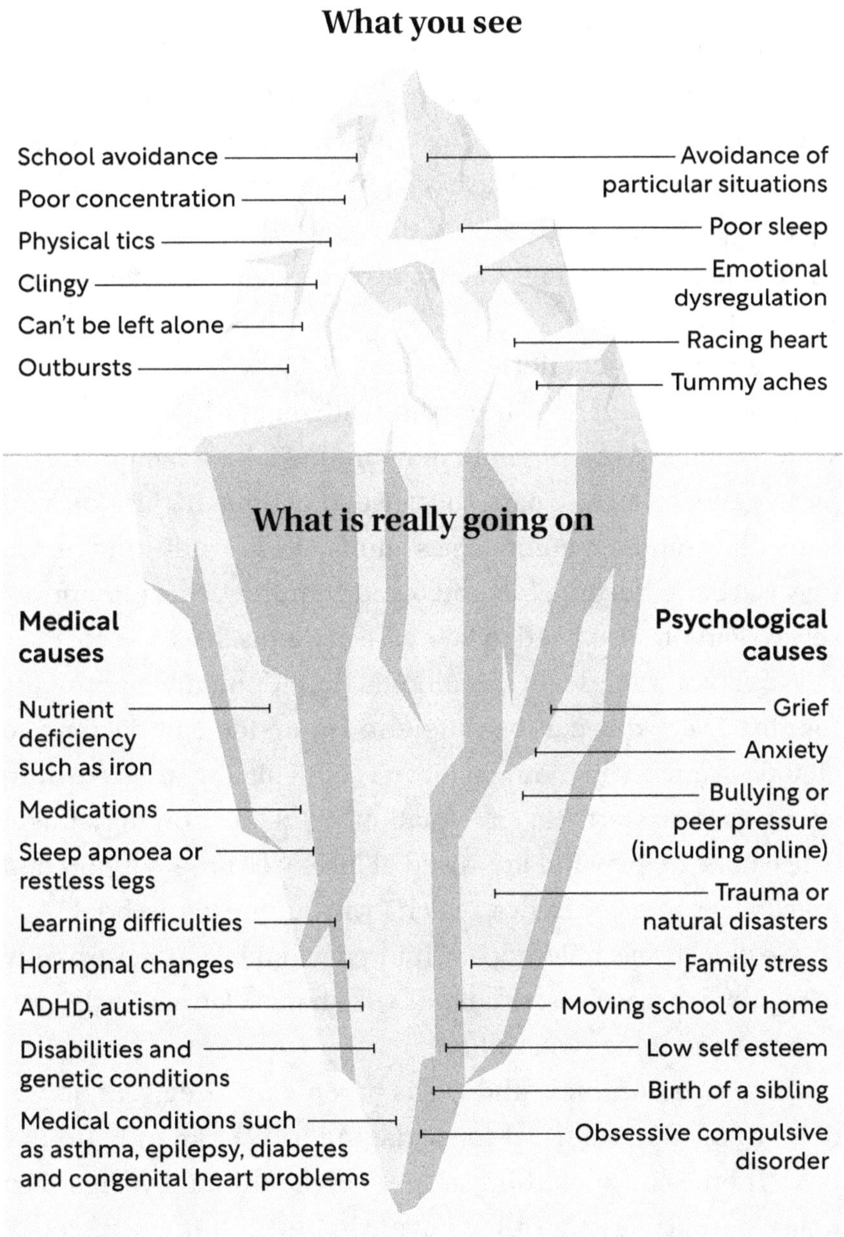

What you see

- School avoidance
- Poor concentration
- Physical tics
- Clingy
- Can't be left alone
- Outbursts
- Avoidance of particular situations
- Poor sleep
- Emotional dysregulation
- Racing heart
- Tummy aches

What is really going on

Medical causes

- Nutrient deficiency such as iron
- Medications
- Sleep apnoea or restless legs
- Learning difficulties
- Hormonal changes
- ADHD, autism
- Disabilities and genetic conditions
- Medical conditions such as asthma, epilepsy, diabetes and congenital heart problems

Psychological causes

- Grief
- Anxiety
- Bullying or peer pressure (including online)
- Trauma or natural disasters
- Family stress
- Moving school or home
- Low self esteem
- Birth of a sibling
- Obsessive compulsive disorder

seem minor to us can be huge for a child. For example, I've seen children one year on after losing their pet dog, still unable to cope with emotional dysregulation.

Of course, anxiety and stress can be a normal and important body response helping us to recognise unsafe or troubling situations. During school tests, class presentations and preparation for exams, the cortisol release is higher in the brain to help drive us to prepare, focus and achieve our goals. This type of anxiety or stress is normal and does not usually lead to problematic anxiety if it's well-managed.

Children are incredibly susceptible to the world around them. If the adults in their lives are dealing with mental health disorders such as anxiety, it's possible that child will be affected. This is partly genetic, but also partly because sometimes it's just too hard to regulate our own emotions as adults. We are only human. We may yell back, become frustrated and withdraw from our normal selves. Parents also need to take care of themselves.

A child or adolescent's emotional development can progress rapidly. Every day can be different. Home life can become so chaotic at any given moment that it is difficult for parents to even know where to start. But any situation, no matter how big it might feel, can be helped and improved. It just takes time, support and practising some key basics, which I will outline in this book.

We can always hold hope. Children will develop more ability to regulate themselves, situations will change, families will learn to adapt and things will settle.

Anxiety is complex, and we as parents or caregivers do not need to try to be perfect in managing it. We can only do our best. There is no such thing as 'perfect parenting'. I've heard so many parents say that they have tried everything: time outs, hugging, not hugging, distractions and so on. They're often on the verge of breaking down themselves. Parents also know their child better than anyone else. No one can tell you how to parent your own child. You won't always get it right. You don't *have* to always get it right. You will figure this out. Children are also very good at figuring *you* out and pushing your buttons when you feel tired at the end of the day. They can challenge us in so many ways, and we ourselves might end up developing anxiety from trying to help.

That said, we as adults need to try to model how we want our children to react in and perceive the world. This means sometimes managing our own anxiety for the sake of our child so that they can develop their own ideas around a situation. This is probably one of the hardest things to do as a parent: to demonstrate and teach our children new ways of dealing with feelings, while managing our own. It is important for parents with anxiety disorders to seek their own help and treatment plan so that they can be as present with their child as possible when their child is going through anxiety symptoms. If we over-react to a situation and start showing panic or yelling at others because they did something that frustrated us, our children will learn from this and think it is okay to yell when they aren't getting what they want. If you do lose control of your emotions, talk to your child and to let them know that you were feeling stressed at the time and they haven't done anything wrong. This teaches them that you have your own vulnerabilities and that you are doing the best you can.

What causes anxiety, and how can we manage it?

There isn't usually a single factor that leads to a child developing anxiety or an anxiety disorder, but a combination of multiple influences over time. Some children will develop anxiety for no reason, it's simply their emotions taking over and their feelings becoming too much. Anxiety is part of our genetic make-up. What 'switches on' that particular gene and how a child copes when it does become more active is still an area of research. One process that has been shown to lead to mental health difficulties in children is trauma. Trauma can be so many things for different people. The more significant the trauma, the more likely an anxiety disorder will develop. A child who has a secure attachment base with at least one person in their life who provides them with a loving bond is better able to cope with stress than a child who experiences neglect. We'll delve into the potential causes in more detail in Part I of this book.

Findings from a 2022 poll as part of the Royal Children's Hospital National Child Health Poll shed light on how families with young children understand and deal with mental health issues. The findings emphasised the importance of education so that parents can identify the warning signs and seek out early intervention. Of the 2000 parents surveyed in the poll:

- One-third believed that mental health problems in kids will 'work themselves out' over time.
- About a quarter did not know that physical symptoms can be signs of mental health problems.
- Fewer than half felt confident about where they could get professional help.[3]

These numbers may seem surprising, particularly if you know that the proportion of children experiencing mental health challenges is at an all-time high. Mental health disorders among young people have soared by nearly 50 per cent in 15 years, new data shows, and the health system is struggling to cope with the growing complexity and demand.

The latest data from the Australian Bureau of Statistics (ABS) shows nearly 40 per cent of young Australians aged 16 to 24 – more than 1 million people – experienced a mental health disorder in the previous year, up from 26 per cent in 2007.[4] The figures show young women were particularly affected, with nearly half (45.5 per cent) experiencing a mental health condition in the previous year, up from 30.1 per cent in 2007. That was compared to one-third of young men (32.4 per cent) up from in 22.8 per cent in 2007. Anxiety disorders were the most common condition, experienced by two in five young women and one in four young men.

But the warning signs and symptoms of mental illness or emotional problems can be hard to identify. According to Dr Anthea Rhodes, Founding Director of the poll, 'Kids are always changing and parents can wonder, is it just another phase or is it something that I need to worry about it?' While the line can be blurry, it's when the challenges are interfering with a child's daily life that concern should shift to action. Some things do get better simply with time, and we don't want to over-catastrophise a situation and potentially worsen it. However, if a child is having ongoing issues that are interfering with their home, school, family or friends or any aspect of life for a couple of months or more, that's when intervention and extra support is needed.

Why I wrote this book

I have noticed a common trend over the last few years since Covid. We are becoming increasingly anxious, with anxiety-related problems representing a large proportion of what I see in consultations. It's unclear whether the acceleration is due to Covid itself or if an increase in anxiety would have occurred regardless. My observation is that we are busier than we can handle. Many of us feel a need to keep ourselves occupied, so we fill our lives with activity and give ourselves very little time to stop and slow down. When we do stop, it can be very difficult to switch off as we are thinking about what we did yesterday, or what we need to do tomorrow.

'Living in the moment' is the antidote to this problem. If we can grasp this concept, we will be on the way to escaping uncomfortable feelings of anxiety. Given we are primed towards planning, organising, working, exercising, meetings and social outings, it takes more effort to reach a sense of fulfillment. What I mean is that we have re-engineered our brains, as a society, to be busier. When we try to stop or slow down, our brains crave stimulation to feel fulfilled or calm. This is the dopamine response we feel when we do things such as exercising. It feels good.

I wrote this book because I've seen both sides of the problem. While I see parents and their children finding anxiety to be difficult to handle, I've also seen them get through and figure out ways to manage it. I've seen my patients implement whole-of-family solutions such as reducing the number of activities scheduled, to cutting back on work, doing mindfulness together or going for bush walks, through to seeking professional guidance.

I want to provide a sense of hope that things can get better, no matter what you might be going through. Sometimes it feels like anxiety will never go away. It is a horrible feeling, but nothing lasts forever. This feeling will pass.

I also hope to demonstrate what the research says: that managing anxiety with effective strategies leads to better physical and mental health outcomes. If we can improve a child's mental health, we can change the trajectory of their entire life.

PART I
UNDER-STANDING ANXIETY

CHAPTER 1

What is Anxiety?

Anxiety is a human emotion that all of us experience. It exists on a continuum, from mildly stressed (one-out-of-10 anxiety) to a panic attack (10-out-of-10 anxiety).

It's common to go through times in which anxiety is towards the higher end of that scale – where it becomes an all-encompassing experience that affects all parts of life. I have experienced this kind of anxiety myself. It felt horrible at the time – like a tight knot in the middle of my chest that wouldn't disappear. The anxiety made me feel sick at times, and I struggled with muscle tension, headaches and poor sleep. It made me think that small things would become big things (this is known as catastrophising). The worst part was that when I tried to do the right thing by relaxing with quiet music and mindfulness, the anxiety became worse.

What worked for me was a combination of treatments, but it took time to figure this out. I found that medication (an SSRI or 'antidepressant') helped with the physical symptoms. It took away the muscle tension, nausea, stomach aches and racing heart. Medication allowed me to get on with doing all those other good things that help anxiety. Anxiety can feel so overwhelming that doing all the good things, such as talking to a psychologist and meditating, are not enough to reduce the fight-or-flight response and chemical component to anxiety. To treat this part we need to include medication in our treatment plan.

Once the physical symptoms abated I was able to exercise more effectively, which is a significant part of how I manage my anxiety even today. Going for a run or bike ride or lifting some weights can all help with mental illness. Soon I felt comfortable talking to a psychologist and undergoing cognitive behavioural therapy (CBT). This form of therapy helps to manage those catastrophic thoughts – the ones that make us feel there is no way through, that everything is awful and we are stuck in this position forever. Psychologists help us to reframe our unhelpful thoughts. This literally rewires our brain so that when that thought comes about again, we don't jump to believing it's the disaster it once was. The psychological help made me a better husband, father and doctor, because I was calmer, less reactive and more present.

Anxiety is an uncomfortable emotion that affects every person differently. Some of us will internalise this feeling, making us feel tense, on edge, tight in the muscles, or racy. Others will externalise, which can lead to panic, fast breathing, fast thoughts or saying something we don't mean to.

Anxiety is meant to protect us from danger. It is meant to warn us that something bad is about to take place. Typically, anxiety is triggered by stress. This is how our brain is programmed to operate. When we are under threat, we have a flight-or-fight experience, driving us to run, feel uneasy, develop a faster heart rate or react in a certain way. This has always been a useful protective mechanism to keep us safe from danger.

ENCOURAGE YOUR CHILD TO BE BRAVE! KNOW THAT IT IS OKAY FOR THEM TO EXPLORE AND TAKE RISKS.

However, the current world is faster and more complicated than ever before, which means it is also more stressful. It can be difficult to strike a balance between finding peace and space in a day filled with work, school and after-school activities.

All children are born with different personality and temperamental traits, which may explain why some children really struggle and others breeze through stress. I see this all the time when I give a child an injection. I've had siblings who are clearly parented the same way, yet both react completely different to the pain of a needle.

I always feel anxious when I speak in front of a room full of people. I start to sweat, my mouth goes dry and my heart starts racing. Somehow, I get through it, and overcome that emotion to be able to complete the talk. I feel relief or happiness after completing a difficult task. We will never change, unless we challenge our thinking.

Your child might feel anxious when they are about to do a running race, or their NAPLAN or school exams. These feelings are normal.

Anxiety and the brain

While there is no need for you to understand the complexities of what is happening in your child's brain when they're feeling anxious, basic foundational knowledge can help you to support your child and understand what they are dealing with.

Various regions of the brain contribute to the processing and regulation of emotions. One key structure is the limbic system, which includes the amygdala, hippocampus, hypothalamus, and cingulate gyrus. The amygdala is often considered a key player in processing emotions, especially fear and pleasure.

That said, it's important to note that emotions are highly interconnected and involve multiple brain regions working together. The brain doesn't have a single 'emotions centre'. The frontal lobe, especially the prefrontal cortex, is crucial for regulating and expressing emotions. Additionally, neurotransmitters (messaging packagers) such as serotonin, dopamine, and noradrenaline play a role in modulating emotional experiences.

This is how I like to describe it: imagine the brain has a boss called the 'prefrontal cortex'.

This boss's job is to make sure everything runs smoothly. It oversees the team without having to do every task itself. Its team, known as the 'frontal cortex', does the actual work. Each member has a specific job, much like how each chemical in the brain has a unique role. Usually, if all goes well, the boss can step back and let the team do its thing. But if something goes wrong and disrupts the team, the boss steps in to sort things out.

When a child or teen feels anxious, it's often because there's a mix-up between the boss and the team. Imagine the boss dozes off or isn't paying attention – the team starts overreacting to even the smallest tasks, with no one to say, 'Slow down.' This can lead to chaos. The team members might be confused and rushing, and making mistakes because they're not getting the right instructions.

Mindfulness and taking things slowly can help strengthen the relationship between the boss and the team, ensuring they can communicate clearly again. Reducing stress and being more 'in the moment' also play crucial roles.

Another way to think about it is to imagine a busy freeway during peak hour. If there's a car accident, traffic that normally flows smoothly across four lanes might get squeezed into just one. This causes a ripple effect: what was once a fast drive becomes a slow, stressful crawl.

In the brain, any upsetting event – like an accident on the freeway – can disrupt the normal flow of messages. For example, trauma, ongoing health issues or being bullied can impact how well the brain's boss and team communicate. This can make a child more likely to feel anxious about things that used to be no big deal.

Young brains have an amazing ability to adapt called neuroplasticity. This means that their brains are still forming connections and will continue doing so until about the age of 25. Although our brains can still change after this age, most nerve connections for child development are formed by this age. This is similar to laying train tracks. The tracks are solid and strong for trains to run over, but they can be altered over time to run new train lines and extend services. Therefore, even if your child is experiencing anxiety, with the right support and treatment, their brain can learn new, healthier ways to respond to the world throughout their life.

What does anxiety look like?

There is a wide variation in how anxiety might present across all age groups. It's common for parents to wonder whether a child is suffering from anxiety, or if what they are experiencing is 'normal' for their child's developmental age. For example, a toddler having multiple meltdowns a day can be normal. A primary-aged child having nightmares and sleepwalking can also be normal. Feeling anxious, stressed, angry or scared are normal parts of growing up and learning about the world.

Researchers at the University of California identified some of the more common situations in which children will experience anxiety as a normal emotional response.[5] These include:

Infancy and toddlerhood (age zero to three)
- Separation
- Stranger shyness

Childhood (age three to six)
- Dying and death of others

- Thunder, lightening, fires, water, darkness, nightmares, animals, imaginary creatures

School age (age six to 12)
- Germs, getting ill, natural disasters, traumatic events, harm to self or others
- School anxiety, performance anxiety

Adolescence (age 12 onwards)
- Fear of negative evaluation
- Peer rejection

Anxiety presents in a variety of ways and can be quite different in children than it is in adults. Quite often, children express their anxiety as a behaviour rather than through words. Sometimes as parents we don't even realise our child is anxious. It can appear that they are playing up or being 'naughty' and defiant, when really they are suffering.

According to the Royal Children's Hospital Melbourne, the following are some signs of anxiety in primary-aged children:

- Avoiding everyday situations
- Difficulty sleeping
- Headaches or tummy aches
- Being preoccupied
- Overplanning
- Changes in appetite
- Seeking reassurance often
- Tantrums or meltdowns.[6]

Following are some of the behaviours parents have told me their child exhibits when they are anxious:

- Becomes shy, nervous or quiet
- Clingy, holding hands, holding leg, crying
- Extremely emotional and teary
- Hurts others for attention
- Displays anger and rage or is short-fused
- Asks lots of questions
- Emotionally dysregulated
- Fingers in mouth
- Looking for parents
- Makes excuses for everything
- Seeks attention.

In the primary school years, most children are not developmentally ready to express their emotions. This varies from child to child. Most will understand what it's like to feel sad, happy and worried, but many will struggle to figure out why they might feel this way. It is up to us adults to explore children's inner emotions by prompting them, giving them some examples of what makes you feel anxious, normalising this emotion and showing that you are ready to listen.

I often hear from parents of children in the early primary years struggling to cope with their child's emotional regulation. Often a child cannot express their anxiety adequately, so after a difficult day at school they might come home and be completely dysregulated. The underlying cause could simply be hunger or being tired. It could also be that they feel different, are falling behind, have troubled friendships or are being bullied. This is why some further exploration can help you determine what is going on. If the behaviour is persistent and difficult to manage, a psychologist or occupational therapist can help to determine what is triggering it.

Children with anxiety may also be simply exhausted by the end of the day from trying so hard with their work and to make friends. Imagine a bottle of soft drink being shaken all day long. Eventually when the lid is taken off there will be an explosion! I use this analogy with kids I see. Another example is a pressure cooker, or a volcano.

Anxiety across the age groups

Let's take a more detailed look at how anxiety can present across different age groups.

Babies

Identifying anxiety in babies can be challenging as they can't express how they feel in words. They may show some signs of discomfort or distress through their behaviours. In saying this, all babies will have periods where they might be unhappy and seem to be excessively crying. It is also quite normal for babies to have a sense of 'stranger danger' when separated from their parent or caregiver. It can take many months for a baby to grow out of this developmental behaviour.

Some symptoms babies might show when experiencing anxiety include:

— **CLINGINESS:** An anxious baby may become excessively clingy and seek constant physical contact and reassurance from their parents or caregivers.

- **CRYING AND FUSSINESS:** While crying is a normal way for babies to communicate, an anxious baby might cry more frequently and intensely, often without an obvious reason. In saying this, many babies do 'just cry'. I have observed that approximately 30 per cent of babies experience excessive crying. This can be due to anxiety, but sometimes it's difficult to pinpoint the reason. This can cause a lot of stress for parents. However, I want to reassure you that babies who cry a lot usually get better with time. Interestingly, these babies often become less agitated and calmer as they grow up. Although there is no scientific data to support this, I observe this change in temperament in the children I work with. Nonetheless, if you are concerned about your baby crying excessively, you should consult a health professional to rule out any underlying medical condition.
- **TROUBLE SLEEPING:** Anxiety can disrupt a baby's sleep patterns, leading to difficulty falling asleep, frequent waking or restless sleep. Our eldest child was one of these babies. She only slept with one of us lying next to her, or with loud white noise turned on! She is now a very happy 10-year-old child with minimal anxiety. Again, what might seem to be a very anxious baby may not lead to long-term emotional problems in that child.
- **FEEDING DIFFICULTIES:** An anxious baby may have trouble feeding and may exhibit signs of discomfort or refusal to eat.
- **LIMITED EXPLORATION:** An anxious baby may be hesitant to explore their surroundings and may prefer to stay close to their primary caregiver.

Babies go through various developmental stages, and their behaviour may change due to natural growth and adjustment. Occasional fussiness and clinginess are common in babies and do not necessarily indicate anxiety.

Younger children (ages four to 11)

Behavioural changes such as lashing out, irritability, crying frequently, poor sleep patterns, crying, clinging during separation such as drop-off at Kindy or school, poor concentration or attention, being more withdrawn and less interactive with others such as children their own age, reduced socialisation with others or avoidance of play are some examples of anxiety. Other examples include:

- **EXCESSIVE WORRY:** Young children with anxiety may worry excessively about a wide range of everyday issues, such as school, friendships, performance or safety.
- **PERFECTIONISM:** Younger children with anxiety might display perfectionist tendencies, becoming overly upset if they make a mistake or cannot meet their own high standards. They can scrunch up a piece of work they might have completed or become frustrated, annoyed and angry when a simple error is made.
- **REGRESSION:** Some children might display regressive behaviours, such as reverting to previously outgrown habits such as thumb-sucking or baby talk.
- **EXCESSIVE SEEKING OF REASSURANCE:** Anxious children may repeatedly ask for reassurance or seek validation from parents or caregivers to alleviate their worries temporarily.

- **PHYSICAL COMPLAINTS:** Anxiety can often manifest as physical symptoms, such as stomach aches, headaches, fatigue, muscle tension or general aches and pains.

It is so important that your GP, paediatrician or child health nurse considers any medical causes of these symptoms before attributing them to anxiety.

Anxiety is certainly a big cause of tummy issues in children, and I see a lot of children with abdominal pain. In my experience as a GP, constipation is a factor in around 70 per cent of all cases of abdominal pain. The challenge here is that children are generally not able to describe their stool patterns, and parents eventually tune out of hearing about their child's toileting habits. So, constipation can go unnoticed for months, even years, until accidents start to occur or there are other issues emerging such as bedwetting.

Picking up anxiety alongside this other common cause of tummy pain can be tricky. I have found that the same children who have chronic constipation are often at risk of anxiety, simply because the constipation leads to anxiety around toileting. These children are naturally more anxious about going to the toilet and potentially having issues in school or public settings. Therefore, treating the physical causes can improve psychological wellbeing as doing so alleviates the fear or worry associated with things such as toileting or going to sleep at night.

If constipation is suspected in any child, I strongly suggest a review with your GP. There are very good stool softeners available over the counter (osmolax, movicol and actilax) which can alleviate this problem. These are all safe and can be used long-term or for however long it takes to get back to a daily 'soft serve' stool action, which is the gold standard!

Other causes of abdominal pain can be found on the RCH website: www.rch.org.au/kidsinfo/fact_sheets/Abdominal_pain

Older children and teens (ages 12 to 18)

We are a product of our parents, and the teens I see who struggle with anxiety often have anxious parents. I see it when I talk to them. As parents it is easy to let our worries get in the way of peace and calm. It is easy to catastrophise what is going on for us and forget about the present moment. But, as adults, this is something we can work on – particularly so that we can avoid passing on these worries to our children.

Young people don't necessarily have the tools just yet to manage their emotions. What might start as a thought about a complicated friendship can become a feeling of being overwhelmed and not wanting to go to school. This is not to say anxiety is abnormal. The sense of fear is a helpful warning when we are under stress, and I tell teens this. But it's also important to teach them to observe and address that warning sign with their support network.

Teens don't show anxiety in the same way as adults. How anxiety manifests varies massively from teen to teen. I ask about anxiety in all young people, and I am always surprised if there is a time that they haven't experienced it for an extended period.

Anxiety in young people, as with younger children, can present as a behaviour rather than an emotion. It can look like situation avoidance, yelling and screaming due to being overwhelmed, self-harming to escape, having a panic attack in the toilet cubicle at school, and even running away. I also see teens later in the journey of anxiety where it has become so escalated they don't know how to regulate their feelings, and often the whole family describes 'walking on eggshells'.

Older children and teenagers generally display behavioural changes that can be particularly challenging to parents. These can include anger, lashing out, yelling and screaming, physical violence to property or to others, self-harm, excessive worry, disrupted sleep, low energy, perfectionism, poor concentration at school or dropping of grades. Other examples of adolescent anxiety include:

- **PHYSICAL SYMPTOMS:** Just as in younger children, anxiety can manifest as physical complaints in adolescents, including headaches, stomach aches, muscle tension, trembling, sweating, dizziness or a racing heart.
- **AVOIDANCE BEHAVIOURS:** Teens with anxiety may avoid situations, places or activities that trigger their anxiety. This could include avoiding social events, school or other activities they once enjoyed. Some teens I see turn this avoidance into fun activities at home such as gaming. They become so entrenched in gaming that it becomes their new normal and nothing else going on outside home or school is as exciting anymore.
- **SUBSTANCE ABUSE:** Some adolescents may turn to drugs or alcohol to cope with their anxiety, leading to potential substance abuse problems. This may not always be obvious. Keeping an open and non-judgemental dialogue when dealing with your teen can help mitigate this becoming worse. While it is so hard, teenagers are easily influenced by those around them and can naturally fall into a trap of risk-taking behaviour to self-treat their emotions. This can be addictive. Teens need support from parents, teachers and healthcare providers to navigate

this and make better decisions for their mental health.
- **NEGATIVE SELF-IMAGE:** Anxiety can contribute to negative self-perception, leading to feelings of inadequacy, self-doubt or low self-esteem. This can put teens at risk of eating disorders as they start to compare themselves to others online (on social media) or in their friendship groups. Eating disorders commonly lead to anxiety. The two issues are closely linked, and eating disorders are more common in girls than boys.
- **PANIC ATTACKS:** Some adolescents with anxiety may experience panic attacks, characterised by sudden and intense feelings of fear, accompanied by physical symptoms such as chest pain, shortness of breath and a sense of impending doom.
- **OBSESSIVE-COMPULSIVE BEHAVIOURS:** In some cases, anxiety can lead to the development of obsessive-compulsive behaviours, where teens engage in repetitive rituals or thoughts to alleviate their anxiety temporarily.

Many children simply need time and support to help them navigate these feelings. This might mean a combination of reassurance, acknowledging the child is going through a challenging time, informing important others such as the child's educator or any other caregivers, and trying not to avoid the triggers altogether.

CHAPTER 2
What Causes Anxiety?

Children's brains are shaped by their environment and genetic make-up from the moment they're born.

I have encountered many children and adolescents suffering from anxiety over the years, and I have observed several common trends that lead to the development of severe or crippling anxiety. Triggers such as life stress, overuse of screens, poor sleep, substance abuse, trauma, bullying and strong family history are the most common. Known factors that increase a child's risk of developing anxiety include a strong family history, stress during pregnancy, stress and anxiety in the early years, trauma, and a stressful upbringing due to problems such as drug and alcohol addiction.

An essential and often overlooked risk factor for childhood anxiety is the mental health of the parents. Anxiety is genetic, and parents who struggle with anxiety tend to display this behaviourally in different situations without understanding the consequences on their children. A typical example of this is the morning school rush. Sometimes, when making school lunches, getting the kids dressed, finding their shoes, packing bags and driving off, we may become anxious. We may raise our voices at our kids or drive through traffic faster than usual, trying to make up those precious lost minutes. This kind of behaviour only puts everyone on edge.

Instead, we can develop an attitude of organisation to leave on time. With a better system or routine where our tasks are clearly laid out on the wall, a timer that reminds us 10 minutes then five minutes out from leaving, and some planning the night before, we should be better equipped to leave on time. Sometimes we may run late, which is inevitable, and this is where we need to show that we can manage our emotions. Coping with stress is an important aspect of helping our children.

Given how unique each child is, the cause of their anxiety will never just be 'one thing'. The cause is multifactorial – that is, a blend of multiple factors. The job for parents and healthcare professionals isn't so much figuring out the cause, but figuring out how this child's anxiety has become severe enough to impact their ability to function. We don't always know what causes this emotion to become difficult to handle. Sometimes it is easier to treat the anxiety as a first step rather than trying to hypothesise about where it is coming from. Usually in this process we figure out the key drivers and in doing this it becomes easier to tackle them.

One important factor that can reduce the risk of developing anxiety is providing a child with the scaffolding, foundations, and skills to manage their emotions, so that when they do experience anxious feelings, they have some strategies to handle them. A child's early life provides the opportunity to do this through play, connection and bonding, helping them through adversity and allowing them to take safe risks.

Anxiety can occur on its own and also as part of other conditions. A GP or paediatrician can usually exclude most of these conditions with a thorough physical examination and blood test. For a child with persistent anxiety I use a comprehensive checklist that screens for medical and psychological causes. Without being thorough like this, we cannot fully understand why our children might be having trouble managing their emotions.

Let's look at some of the contributing factors in more detail.

Genetics

Genetic factors can play a role in predisposing some children to be more susceptible to anxiety. Children with a family history of anxiety disorders may have a higher likelihood of experiencing anxiety themselves.

Environmental stress and traumatic experiences

Stressful life events, such as moving to a new school, parental divorce, loss of a loved one or witnessing traumatic events can trigger feelings of anxiety in children.

Trauma can occur at any time and to various levels of severity. In a clinical context we call traumatic experiences adverse childhood experiences (ACEs). These experiences can include physical, emotional, or sexual abuse; neglect; household dysfunction, such as substance abuse, mental illness or domestic violence; and other forms of adversity. The Adverse Childhood Experiences study, conducted by the Centers for Disease Control and Prevention (CDC) and Kaiser Permanente, demonstrated a correlation between the number of ACEs a person experiences and their risk of various health and social problems later in life.[7] Understanding and addressing ACEs is crucial for promoting resilience and preventing the long-term negative effects of childhood trauma.

For high-risk groups such as children affected by violence, abuse, maltreatment or poverty, early intervention can help reduce disparities between the mental health of these children and children in psychologically healthy environments.[8]

Parenting style

Parental behaviour and parenting style can influence a child's anxiety levels. Overprotective or excessively critical parenting can contribute to a child's anxiety, as can inconsistent or unpredictable parenting. This is why it is crucial we 'relax' some of our parenting 'rules' to allow for flexibility. Rigid, rules-based parenting can be detrimental when it comes to anxiety.

School pressure

Academic demands, social pressures and school-related stressors can contribute to anxiety in children. Performance expectations, test anxiety and social interactions can all be stressful to young people. Children with perfectionistic traits certainly have more risk of anxiety. When things don't go their way or they get an unexpected grade, it is not uncommon to notice them react to this with emotional distress. Resilience-building will help them, and we'll discuss this later in the book.

It is important to teach children how to handle failure in a positive way. For instance, when a child falls off their bike and gets hurt, how do you react? Do you panic and become anxious, or do you stay calm and help your child get back up? Your reaction in this situation can teach your child how to respond to challenges in life. By remaining calm, caring and positive, you can help your child build resilience and learn to deal with difficult situations. On the other hand, if you show a sense of losing control and become stressed, your child may perceive the situation as dangerous and stressful as well. It is possible to teach children emotional intelligence in the early stages of brain development, so it is important to be mindful of how we react to challenges in front of them.

Lack of social connection

Difficulties in making friends or experiencing social rejection can cause anxiety in children, as can bullying or peer rejection.

The media and social media

Exposure to frightening or violent content in the media can also contribute to anxiety in sensitive children. Similarly, excessive social media use and the inability to switch off from this can contribute.

Personality traits

Children with certain personality traits, such as being perfectionistic, shy or more sensitive, may be more prone to experiencing anxiety.

Psychological conditions

Some psychological conditions are also linked with anxiety. Let's take a look at those now.

Post-traumatic stress disorder (PTSD)

Trauma can exist in many forms, and each of us, including children, experience trauma in different ways, which is why we cannot underestimate any negative or difficult experience a child might be going through. Some examples of trauma that might not be considered include being bullied at school, the death of a loved one or pet, being isolated from social settings or family, or going to the hospital for a procedure or an injury. The ability to cope with traumatic events such as these depends on that child's personality traits, resilience and ability to process the event, their age and how much support they might receive.

Children present with behavioural changes after a traumatic event, such as being angry, defiant or withdrawn. Early intervention regardless of the extent of the trauma has the greatest benefit on children's mental wellbeing. This intervention is likely to be a combination of play therapy with an occupational therapist (OT) or psychologist, parenting strategies, cognitive behavioural therapy (CBT) and eye movement desensitisation and reprocessing (EMDR), depending on your child's age.

CASE STUDY

LUCAS'S STORY OF RECOVERY   Age: 10

Background

Lucas is a bright and curious child who lives with his mother and younger sister in a close-knit suburb. He enjoys school, particularly science and maths, and plays soccer on the weekends. Last year, Lucas was in a car accident. He was a passenger while his aunt was driving. Although he suffered only minor physical injuries, his aunt was seriously hurt and hospitalised for several weeks. The event was highly distressful and has deeply impacted him.

Lucas is experiencing the following:

- **Excessive worry:** Lucas often expresses concerns about his family members' safety when they are not home. He frequently asks for reassurance that his loved ones are safe and becomes anxious when he cannot see or communicate with them immediately.
- **Reluctance to travel:** Since the accident, Lucas is hesitant to ride in cars, particularly on the freeway or in heavy traffic. He feels trapped and unsafe in a car.
- **Physical symptoms:** He experiences headaches and stomach aches, particularly during situations that remind him of the accident or when he is feeling more anxious than usual.
- **Sleep disturbances:** Lucas has trouble falling asleep and experiences nightmares about car accidents, which further exacerbate his daytime anxiety.

Parental intervention

- **Acknowledgement and validation:** Lucas's mother always acknowledges his feelings with understanding and empathy.

She reassures him by saying things like, 'It's okay to feel scared about that. I'm here with you,' which helps validate his feelings rather than dismissing them.
- **Routine and predictability:** His mother helps Lucas by maintaining a consistent daily routine, which provides him with a sense of stability and predictability. This is especially important on days involving car travel.

Professional support

Recognising the signs of persistent anxiety and sensing the possibility of PTSD, his mother seeks help from a GP, who prepares a mental health treatment plan and refers Lucas to a psychologist. The psychologist is working with Lucas using trauma-focused cognitive behavioural therapy (TF-CBT) to help him process his fears and develop coping strategies.

Education and communication

Lucas's mother educates herself about trauma and anxiety to better understand what Lucas is experiencing. She communicates openly with him about his appointments and what he is learning in therapy, and she encourages him to use relaxation techniques such as deep breathing and visualisation when he feels overwhelmed.

With ongoing therapy, support from his family and a strong routine, Lucas begins to show signs of improvement. He starts to manage short car trips around the local neighbourhood and engages more with his friends and family during outings, slowly reclaiming the joys of his young life.

Lucas's story shows that with the right support and professional help, children can recover and regain a sense of normalcy even after experiencing significant trauma.

Attention-deficit/hyperactivity disorder (ADHD)

Children with ADHD may experience restlessness, impulsivity and difficulty focusing, which can lead to anxiety, especially in academic or social settings.

This can be a 'chicken and egg' scenario. Anxiety can lead to poor concentration and difficulty holding attention at school, which can very much look like ADHD.

Likewise, ADHD can lead to poor school performance, not reaching potential, getting told off at school, and the result can be anxiety. Sometimes treatment will be given to one condition first, to understand which is leading to which.

Autism spectrum disorder (ASD)

Children with autism may experience anxiety due to challenges with social interactions, communication difficulties and sensory sensitivities. It is quite common for children with autism to experience various degrees of anxiety.

Major depressive disorder (MDD)

Children with MDD (depression) may also experience symptoms of anxiety, such as excessive worry and feelings of unease. Again, these two conditions are often linked and difficult to pull apart. The treatments are the same for both. We'll cover this in more detail later in this book.

Adjustment disorders

Significant life changes or stressors can trigger anxiety symptoms in children, leading to an adjustment disorder. These stressors can range from moving house or school to losing a loved one or pet. This anxiety can be experienced over a brief period of time, or for some children appear later and last longer.

Selective mutism

This condition involves a persistent inability to speak in specific social situations, often due to anxiety or fear. I have seen children with selective mutism in our GP office. Understandably, children are shy when they come to a new place or an intimidating environment such as a medical clinic. Selective mutism is more than simply being shy. It is a persistent inability to interact with people the child is unfamiliar with. For example, children I get to know over a few consultations would direct my questions to a parent every visit, regardless of how gentle my approach might be. They tend to be seated on their parent's lap or look away from me and struggle to find the confidence to voice their responses. I recognise that I can't 'force' a child to speak to me in this situation. It often takes much longer to develop trust and rapport but I accept this as part of the therapy and treatment process.

Medical conditions

Acute illnesses that lead to being unwell, poor sleep related to large tonsils or blocked airways, even iron deficiency can contribute to anxiety problems. Chronic conditions such as epilepsy, asthma, diabetes or juvenile arthritis, where a child might feel different, take medication at school, miss school due to the illness or needing to attend appointments, can also play a part. Let's take a look at some of the other medical conditions linked to anxiety.

Thyroid disorders

Both an overactive thyroid (hyperthyroidism) and an underactive thyroid (hypothyroidism) can contribute to anxiety-like symptoms in children. Thyroid hormone imbalances can affect mood and emotional regulation.

Heart problems

Certain heart conditions, such as arrhythmias or heart defects, may cause physiological sensations of anxiety, such as rapid heart rate or palpitations, which can be distressing for children. A GP can screen for this via an electrocardiogram (ECG) and blood pressure check. These are relatively straightforward to do in a GP consultation. An ECG involves a nurse or doctor putting sticky dots on your child's chest. Cords are attached to the sticky dots. These read the electrical rhythm of the heart and provide a tracing. From this we can determine if the heart rate is slow or fast and regular or irregular. A blood pressure check involves wrapping a cuff around your child's arm. This cuff inflates with air, a bit like a balloon. I often tell children it will 'give their arm a hug'. The more relaxed and 'floppy' your child's arm is, the quicker the blood pressure will read. This reading is often lower than what it might be in adults.

Lung problems

Conditions that affect breathing, such as asthma, can lead to feelings of anxiety due to difficulty breathing or a sense of suffocation. Most GP clinics offer spirometry – a simple breathing test that is valid from when your child is aged eight or nine and has the lung capacity to breathe enough air into the machine. It determines very quickly if your child has any signs of asthma or other lung problems, which are important not to miss. Asthma is important to manage well, and all children with problematic asthma should be on a preventer. I have noticed some children who use a lot of Ventolin can feel anxious due to the way Ventolin increases their heart rate. Asthma itself can also be a scary condition as it limits your child's ability to breathe. When a child can't breathe they naturally become panicked and feelings of anxiety are exacerbated.

Gut problems

Digestive issues, such as constipation, irritable bowel syndrome (IBS) or gastroesophageal reflux disease (GORD), can cause physical discomfort and may contribute to anxiety in children.

Likewise, iron or B12 deficiency from inadequate intake of these vitamins (or poor absorption, which can occur with conditions such as coeliac disease) can lead to physical symptoms including fatigue or weakness, which subsequently can lead to anxiety. Recently I have started treating resistant iron deficiency in children with iron infusions. These increase iron levels more rapidly than oral supplements and can be performed in a clinic in less than an hour. I have noticed children who have had their iron levels restored experience increased energy and focus and improved quality of sleep, and, as a result, improved mental health and wellbeing. While many would argue that iron can be adequately restored with oral iron supplements, this can be a slow and difficult process as often the iron won't absorb well, or the oral liquids cause side effects that are not tolerated.

Nerve and brain conditions

Some neurological disorders, such as epilepsy or migraines, can lead to anxiety symptoms because of the impact on brain function and sensory processing. I have been treating a teenager who has had severe epilepsy leading to seizures in class and head injuries. The combination of needing strong and sometimes sedating medication, with the risk of a seizure in a public environment such as in class, can lead to developing anxiety. This boy was incredibly resilient and still managed to get through school without feeling burdened by his seizure disorder. We found that early intervention with a regular psychologist has been helpful in breaking down the difficulties he faces with this, and helping him talk to other teens in class so they understand him better.

Chronic pain conditions

Children experiencing chronic pain conditions, such as juvenile arthritis or fibromyalgia, may develop anxiety as a response to persistent discomfort.

Allergies

Severe allergies or sensitivities to certain foods or environmental triggers may cause anxiety-like reactions in children. If a child is scratching all night from eczema, or coughing and waking up from asthma, they are unlikely to have a decent sleep, leading to fatigue and mental health symptoms in the day.

Also, children with chronic physical conditions may need medication that makes them groggy, have poor sleep, experience low mood or gain or lose weight through appetite changes.

These children may also have frequent visits to medical

settings or hospitals. This may lead to more time out of school, as they are subjected to more tests or investigations and require multiple medications.

Children who are more sensitive may struggle to handle this sort of challenge and need lots of reassurance and support.

Other causes

There are many reasons why a child might develop anxiety. Some of these are unpredictable and not linked to any of the risk factors I've listed here. I still see children with no obvious risk factors develop anxiety. To me this is intriguing, yet we usually find something. These children are probably more prone to anxiety due to genetics, or there is something deeper going on which is important for us to figure out together.

CHAPTER 3

What is an Anxiety Disorder?

Anxiety is an emotion that we all experience in varying intensities on any given day.

Anxiety disorders occur when that emotion becomes a professionally diagnosed medical illness due to the impact it has on your child's life over a particular duration of time.

> **AN ANXIETY DISORDER MAY BE PRESENT IF THE ANXIETY IS BECOMING PERSISTENT AND OVERWHELMING, IS INTERFERING WITH HOME OR SCHOOL, AND IS PREVENTING YOUR CHILD FROM DOING THINGS THEY PREVIOUSLY ENJOYED.**

Anxiety lies on a spectrum from normal worry to transient anxiety, through to severe and disabling symptoms. An anxiety disorder is different to anxiety or worry that comes and goes, or even anxiety that comes after a difficult event such as a grief reaction. For example, children who grieve the loss of a pet or loved one tend to display some anxious feelings. Some children I have seen who have gone through grief have become withdrawn and sensitive. Others have become volatile and reactive. Children can be unpredictable in their responses, and it is difficult to guess how things might play out. For this reason, all we can do is support and reassure our children that this situation will get better, and these feelings are not forever.

If you suspect your child's anxiety symptoms may be moving beyond the day-to-day anxiety we all experience, my advice is to seek help early to figure out the best treatment plan for you and your child.

To be diagnosed with an anxiety disorder according to the Diagnostic and Statistical Manual of Mental Disorders (DSM – the diagnostic manual of psychiatry, which is updated every few years), a child needs to experience disabling anxiety symptoms over at least a two-week period. The DSM uses a set of criteria for both adults and children to help clinicians decide if a child is developing an anxiety disorder rather than simply experiencing episodes of anxiety. While the DSM provides a framework that allows GPs, paediatricians, psychiatrists and psychologists to understand what might be going on for that child, I rarely get hung up in the exact 'label' (especially if the child is listening to the conversation). I find it more beneficial to work on ensuring there is nothing else going on and what might be driving the anxiety so that we can work on some support. I will talk to parents and the child and take a thorough history of what has been going on. It will eventually become apparent whether the problems being faced are interfering with that child's life enough to be deemed an anxiety disorder.

In this way, your GP and other medical professionals can

help you distinguish between anxiety as a symptom or normal reaction and an anxiety disorder (see figure 2), as the treatments can be quite different. Anxiety as a disorder can also cause more significant impact on a child's learning and behaviour.

FIGURE 2: ANXIOUS FEELINGS VERSUS ANXIETY DISORDER

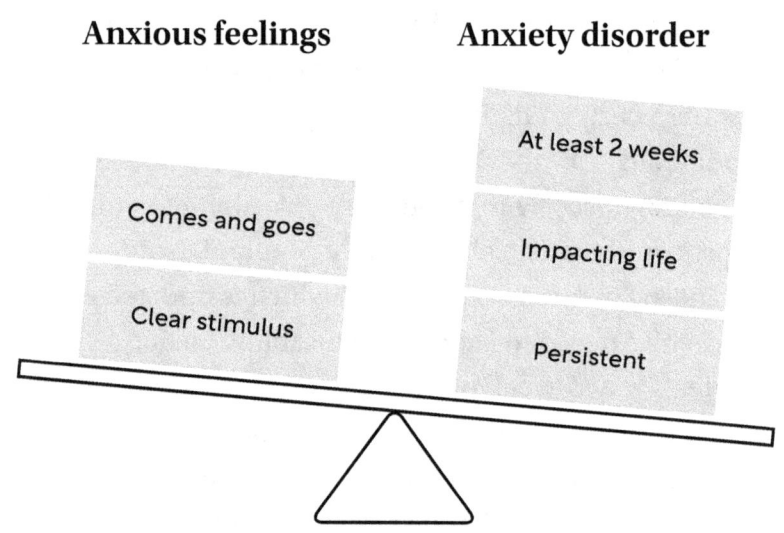

The prevalence and impact of anxiety disorders

The most common anxiety disorder is separation anxiety disorder, affecting more than a quarter of children. ADHD is more common than anxiety disorders, but is not a mental health disorder per se – it is a neurodevelopmental disorder, affecting approximately one in ten children.

The Young Minds Matter Survey is one of the largest performed in Australia to date.[9] The last reported statistics were in 2013–2014, and I can only assume, based on my experience in general practice, we have since seen a rise across all areas of mental health issues in children. The Young Minds Matter Survey indicated that anxiety disorders were the second most common disorders among all children (6.9 per cent). ADHD was the most common disorder for children (8.2 per cent) and the most common among boys (11 per cent). Three in four children had mild anxiety disorders, one in five had moderate disorders and less than one in 10 had severe disorders. This suggests that most children will experience a period of poor mental health, while less than one in 10 will actually receive an anxiety disorder diagnosis. Having a difficult time in our childhood does not necessarily need to lead to a formal diagnosis of a 'disorder'. Some parents will question whether a label is actually needed at such an early age. In terms of getting the right help for more complicated or intrusive symptoms, I find a definition of symptoms to be useful through use of a diagnosis. That is, if a child has persistent worry, avoidance of activities, emotional distress that affects their day to day activity and poor sleep or social interaction, then we need to help psychologists and other doctors understand what we are treating; we need that information to form a diagnosis. For reassurance, I explain to parents that this label is not 'forever'. It is a definition that enables us to understand their child. It is very fluid though and will often change over time.

A more concerning trend revealed by this survey was that only around 49 per cent of children with mental health disorders used services for emotional or behavioural issues.[10] This means there was a gap between children who were struggling, and those who got help. I can hypothesise that there are probably many reasons for this gap. Lack of services in the area (especially in rural and remote areas), lack of awareness of which mental health services can be used, inability to afford those services and stigma. Not wanting to seek help because it might lead to a label or stigma concerns me. GPs are well placed to see any child who might be having a difficult time and I will always encourage parents to bring their child to their GP if they have concerns.

Various research projects have assessed the impact of the Covid-19 pandemic on the mental health of Australia's children. In October 2021, one of these studies found substantial deterioration of children's mental health, particularly during periods of lockdown and for children with pre-existing conditions or families in financial distress.[11]

Looking at more recent data in the US, 9.4% of children aged three to 17 had diagnosed anxiety in 2016–2019.[12] The rates have been steadily increasing over the last 10 years.

Let's now take a look at some of the most common anxiety disorders.

Separation anxiety disorder

Separation anxiety is the most common anxiety disorder. It occurs when kids feel really scared or worried when they are away from their parents or caregivers. They might worry that something bad will happen to their loved ones or that they'll get lost or won't be able to see them again. These feelings can make it tough for them to be apart from their parents, go to school or spend time with friends.

Children with separation anxiety disorder might cry a lot, cling to their parents or refuse to go to places such as school or sleepovers. They may also have physical symptoms such as stomach aches or headaches when they think about being separated from their loved ones.

It's normal for kids to feel sad or upset when they're away from their parents sometimes, but with separation anxiety disorder, these feelings are much stronger and can cause a lot of distress.

Children may miss school because they cannot separate from their parent. Some children genuinely feel they are never going to see their parent again. This can be heightened when there has been a parental separation or death of a parent, leaving the child to feel they will be left with no one to take care of them.

Separation anxiety can be very stressful for the family, as parents are likely to feel guilty about leaving their child crying in a classroom. Most children will eventually settle down and have a good day. There is no right or wrong in this situation and you really need to work with your child's teachers to come up with a plan around what works for your child. If using a step-wise approach, you might spend a set period of time in the classroom with your child before leaving them. Alternatively you might allow your child shorter days and gradually build them up. This needs to be negotiated with the school and figured out in advance so that everyone understands what will happen during school drop-off.

I've seen some school teachers meet children at the gate and walk them into the class. This is a really nice idea and helpful for parents. Not all schools have the resources to do this, however, and you may find yourself walking your child into class for the first few years until they build the confidence to go by themselves. What's important is that they are given the push to become independent and take the next step up the ladder. If the next step up the ladder doesn't work out, go back to the previous step, and try again when they are ready.

Generalised anxiety disorder (GAD)

GAD in children is when kids worry a lot about many different things, even when there's no real reason to be so worried. These worries can be about school, family, friends, health or other everyday things. To the child, the worrying feels like it never goes away, and can make kids feel really stressed and anxious.

GAD typically starts to show when children reach school age. Babies, toddlers and preschoolers usually don't have GAD.

According to the Raising Children Network, if your child has generalised anxiety, they might:

- Continually ask the same questions in new or unfamiliar situations – for example, 'What's going to happen?' or 'What if … ?'
- Worry about a lot of things – for example, health, schoolwork, school or sport performance, money, safety or world events
- Feel the need to be perfect
- Fear asking or answering questions in class
- Find it hard to perform in tests
- Seek constant reassurance.[13]

There are also some physical signs – stomach aches, headaches, tiredness, restlessness and inattention. Children might also spend more than an hour getting to sleep at night, because they're worrying about the events of the next day.

The signs of generalised anxiety can be easy to miss. Your child might work very hard in the classroom and other situations. It can be difficult to know they're constantly worrying.

Children with GAD might find it hard to control their worries, and these worries can be so big that they interfere with their daily life and activities. They might also be perfectionists, always seeking approval, or be really hard on themselves, even when they do things well.

It's essential to remember that it's normal to feel worried or nervous sometimes, but with GAD, the worrying becomes overwhelming and persistent.

There is a common link between anxiety and poor concentration at school. This can be a difficult feeling to differentiate and some childhood educators, parents or doctors can get caught up by thinking this child has ADHD when in fact they have anxiety.

CASE STUDY

SOPHIE'S WORRY LIST   Age: 8

Background

Sophie is an only child living with her parents in an inner city neighbourhood. She attends a local primary school and enjoys art classes and swimming lessons. Despite appearing happy in her activities, Sophie expresses constant worries about things that most of her peers don't seem concerned with. She has been observed to be excessively worried about a variety of things, such as her parents' health, the safety of her home, and her academic performance. Her parents notice that she often asks reassurance questions and seeks comfort multiple times a day about whether things are going to be okay. Sophie has trouble sleeping, frequently waking up from nightmares about losing her parents or her home catching fire.

Her anxiety has led to difficulties concentrating in school, and she often seems distracted or distant. Her teacher has reported that Sophie seems unusually tense during class and is hesitant to participate in group activities for fear of making mistakes or being judged by her peers.

Parental intervention and professional support

After noticing these signs, Sophie's parents consult with their GP and are referred to a child psychologist, who recommends CBT to help Sophie manage her worries.

Sophie's parents also begin setting aside time each day, such as on the way to school, to talk about Sophie's fears, helping her to gradually confront and manage her anxieties in a supportive environment.

Sophie starts a picture journal where she has a safe space to document her feelings in colours and images. She also joins a small, local social group which enables her to reconnect with others in a casual and friendly way.

With a lot of reassurance from her parents, eventually the anxiety feelings ease and she develops her confidence at home and school.

CASE STUDY

MAX'S SCHOOL FEARS   Age: 5

Background

Max is a vibrant and energetic primary school kid who lives with his mother, father and younger sister in an urban setting. He was always eager to explore new activities until his behaviour starts to change.

Max begins to show significant distress about going to school each morning. He complains of stomach aches and often cries, pleading to stay home. At home, he frequently asks his parents if he has to go to school the next day. His mother notices that Max often worries about very unlikely events, such as getting lost at school or the school building collapsing.

Max's anxiety affects his social interactions; he is reluctant to make new friends or engage in play dates, worrying excessively about his parents not returning to pick him up. His teacher has mentioned that Max's anxiety seems to inhibit his engagement with peers and participation in learning activities.

Parental intervention and professional support

Concerned about Max's escalating anxiety, his parents begin working with their GP who refers Max to an occupational therapist (OT) who specialises in childhood anxiety disorders. The OT recommends a combination of play therapy, which will allow Max to express his anxieties in a safe and controlled environment, and parental guidance to help reinforce security and routine at home.

Social anxiety disorder (SAD)

SAD is more than just shyness. It's a common anxiety disorder that affects about 5 per cent of Australian children and adolescents, causing them to feel intense fear in social situations where they might be judged or watched by others.[14]

Children and adolescents with SAD often experience a range of symptoms similar to what we have already explored, ranging from physical through to emotional and behavioural. Physical symptoms might include excessive sweating, trembling, rapid heartbeat, and sometimes nausea or dizziness during social interactions.

There is often intense fear about being embarrassed or humiliated in front of peers, which can lead to extreme nervousness and anxiety when thinking about or being in social situations. You might notice your child starting to avoid activities they once enjoyed, such as birthday parties or school events, out of fear of social interaction. For example:

— Emma, age 12, used to be bubbly and outgoing, but lately, she's been making excuses to avoid sleepovers and birthday parties. Her parents notice she becomes visibly stressed when asked to attend social gatherings.
— Liam, age 15, has always been a strong student, but recently, he's been struggling with school presentations. His anxiety manifests physically; he experiences severe stomach aches and even vomits before he has to present.

While the exact cause of social anxiety disorder is unknown, a combination of genetic, behavioural and environmental factors plays a role. Children with a family history of anxiety are at higher risk, as are those who have experienced bullying or social exclusion. Parenting styles, particularly overprotectiveness, can also contribute to the development of social anxiety.

Strategies for parents include:

- **EDUCATION:** Learning about the symptoms and effects of SAD can help you catch it early. Encourage your child to talk about their feelings and fears without judgement.
- **BEHAVIOURAL STRATEGIES:** Gradually exposing your child to feared situations can be effective. Start small, like a short play date, and build up to larger groups or more challenging interactions.
- **ENCOURAGEMENT:** Positive reinforcement can do wonders. Praise your child for their efforts to face their fears, no matter how small these steps may seem.

Obsessive-compulsive disorder (OCD)

OCD in children is a condition in which kids have recurring thoughts or worries (obsessions) that make them feel very anxious. To cope with this anxiety, they feel compelled to complete certain actions or rituals (compulsions).

For example, a child with OCD might have a strong fear of germs and feel like they'll get sick if they touch something 'dirty'. They may wash their hands repeatedly throughout the day to try to manage that fear. But even after washing their hands, the fear and anxiety may come back, leading them to wash their hands again and again.

These obsessions and compulsions can take up a lot of the child's time and make it challenging for them to do regular activities such as schoolwork or spending time with friends. Sometimes children with OCD know that their thoughts and actions are excessive or don't make sense, but they feel like they have to do them anyway to reduce their anxiety.

OCD is very important to detect. Treatment is generally more involved than for other anxiety disorders and will often include a combination of medication and psychological therapy. Medication may reach higher doses than with other anxiety disorders due to the severity of this condition's impact on a child's daily function, and the intrusiveness of their thought patterns. Parents need to be patient in managing children with OCD. It can be very testing on the whole family.

Here are some examples of how OCD might present:

- **EXCESSIVE HANDWASHING OR CLEANING:** A young person with OCD might feel a constant fear of germs or contamination, leading them to wash their hands excessively or clean objects over and over again.
- **CHECKING RITUALS:** They may have intense worries that they forgot to lock the door, turn off appliances or complete other tasks, causing them to repeatedly check these things to make sure everything is 'right'.
- **INTRUSIVE THOUGHTS:** A young person with OCD may experience distressing and unwanted thoughts, such as fears of harming themselves or others, leading them to engage in rituals to prevent these thoughts from 'coming true'.
- **COUNTING AND ARRANGING:** Some young people may feel compelled to count to a certain number or arrange objects in specific patterns to reduce anxiety.

- **NEED FOR SYMMETRY:** They might feel a strong need for things to be symmetrical or evenly organised, and if things are not 'just right', this can cause significant distress.
- **AVOIDANCE:** Young people with OCD may try to avoid certain situations or places that trigger their obsessions, which can interfere with their social life and normal activities.
- **DIFFICULTY WITH UNCERTAINTY:** Young people with OCD may struggle to tolerate uncertainty and engage in rituals as a way to gain a false sense of control and certainty.

CASE STUDY

ELLA'S ENDLESS CHECKING — Age: 13

Background

Ella is a Year 8 student living in a small town with her parents and younger brother. She has always been a high achiever and meticulous in her schooling. Over the past year, her behaviours have escalated into anxiety-driven compulsions.

Ella develops a routine that involves repeatedly checking the locks on doors and windows each night, often going through the checking process more than a dozen times before she feels secure enough to go to bed. She expresses a persistent fear that if she doesn't perform these checks, something terrible will happen to her family.

Her rituals extend her bedtime significantly, sometimes keeping her up until early morning, which affects her sleep and concentration in school. Ella's parents notice her grades dropping and her mood becoming increasingly irritable and anxious.

Parental Intervention and professional support

After recognising that Ella's behaviours were beyond typical thoroughness, her parents visit their GP and are referred to a paediatric psychiatrist.

Ella is diagnosed with OCD and begins exposure and response prevention (ERP) therapy, a form of CBT specifically effective for OCD, with a child psychologist. Her parents also attend sessions to learn how to support Ella at home without accommodating her compulsions, encouraging her to gradually face her fears and reduce the checking behaviour.

CASE STUDY

LIAM'S RITUALS OF ORDER   Age: 7

Background

Liam lives in an apartment in a bustling city with his parents and twin sister. He is a curious and imaginative second grader who enjoys drawing and building models. However, his need for order and symmetry has grown into compulsive behaviours.

Liam insists that all his personal items be arranged in perfect symmetry and becomes extremely upset if his order is disturbed. He spends a lot of time organising his toys and books every day after school, refusing to do homework or play until everything is aligned. He also performs certain rituals before eating, such as aligning all his utensils at right angles.

These compulsions are time-consuming and cause significant distress, leading to frequent meltdowns if his parents get in the way and pack things up. This is also affecting his social interactions and schoolwork. His parents are unsure how to handle his distress when his routines are interrupted.

Parental intervention and professional support

Concerned about the disruption to Liam's daily life and his emotional wellbeing, his parents seek help from a psychologist who confirms an OCD diagnosis.

They began a treatment plan that includes therapy sessions focused on CBT for Liam, and guidance for his parents on how to reduce accommodation of his compulsions and set gentle but firm limits around his rituals.

Avoidant/restrictive food intake disorder (ARFID)

This is a feeding or eating disorder characterised by an apparent lack of interest in eating or food, avoidance based on the sensory characteristics of food, or concerns about the adverse consequences of eating. Unlike with other eating disorders such as anorexia nervosa or bulimia nervosa, children with ARFID do not have concerns about their body weight or shape.

ARFID often manifests in early childhood, and individuals with this disorder may exhibit selective eating habits, limited food preferences, avoidance of certain textures or smells, and a reluctance to try new foods. This can lead to nutritional deficiencies, weight loss and impaired social functioning.

Treatment for ARFID typically involves a multidisciplinary approach, including medical, nutritional and psychological interventions. Nutritional counselling, exposure therapy to gradually increase food variety, and addressing any underlying anxiety or sensory issues are common components of treatment.

Neurodiversity (ADHD and autism)

Anxiety disorders and neurodiversity generally overlap and coexist. However, a child with anxiety does not always have ADHD, and vice versa. This is why it can be tricky for health professionals to weed out the underlying cause of your child's difficulties.

It's common for a child with neurodiversity to present with anxiety as a result of the difficulties they are experiencing due to their neurodivergence (for example, difficulty concentrating at school), which affects their self-esteem. Feedback from others can make them feel self-conscious or bring awareness to their limitations.

Some children work extremely hard to keep up, especially in early primary years, and fly under the radar, seeming to be on track at school but becoming highly emotional at home. This is a bit like a pressure cooker effect. The pressure builds up all day until the child is home in their place of comfort, where they explode – just like the shaken-up soft drink bottle analogy I used earlier in the book. This is why it can be important to explore a child's school life by speaking to their teachers or asking them how they manage their schoolwork. Some teachers may not see the subtle signs of a child who is not reaching their potential. In this situation, arranging an independent academic and IQ assessment through an educational psychologist can help you understand where your child might be performing compared to their true potential.

Anxiety disorders are usually easier to diagnose when they exist in isolation, especially when there is no other family history of neurodiversity and the child has developed the symptoms later on rather than exhibiting them all the way through childhood. Anxiety can come and go, be more specific to certain situations and have a more recognised pattern.

ADHD and autism have less predictable patterns than anxiety disorders and the signs can be more subtle. They are usually present from early primary school years, but start to emerge more prominently as the pressure of school and social challenges increase. Children may feel left behind but continue to try and keep up. I imagine a duck paddling hard underwater but moving at the same pace above water regardless of how hard they paddle. Children with neurodiversity often work extra hard to keep up to the same pace as everyone else. Eventually there is a tipping point where they can't keep up, and this is where the anxiety begins, and the child may show more emotional symptoms.

This can present in some children as meltdowns, anger, or fatigue on returning home from school as they have held it together all day. It can also present as school avoidance as they don't want to have to try to keep up anymore – their self-esteem and confidence are low.

Autism tends to manifest in social challenges, difficulties reading social cues and maintaining friendships, fixed views and interests, along with the challenges that children with ADHD experience such as low self-esteem and feeling 'different' to others. Children with autism and ADHD are bright and have amazing potential but often don't reach this potential due to their misunderstanding of how to interpret their teachers or tasks. The combination of these issues can lead them to develop anxiety or other mental health struggles.

A screening for ADHD and autism is generally warranted if you suspect your child isn't suffering from straightforward anxiety.

Once ADHD has been diagnosed, treatment with medication such as stimulant-based tablets can have a remarkable effect on their anxiety levels. Children feel much less overwhelmed by their busy brain and are better able to regulate. Stimulant medication can improve symptoms in children with ADHD by 70 to 80 per cent which can be very rewarding when a child has been struggling so much.[15]

Children diagnosed with autism require a multifaceted approach to their treatment. This means looking at all areas they find difficult and managing them together. This might involve a psychologist or behavioural therapist to help with behaviour and emotions, an occupational therapist to help with social skills and motor skills such as writing, or a speech therapist to help develop words and sentences.

CASE STUDY

OLIVER'S CHALLENGES   Age: 6

Background

Oliver is in Year 1 and lives with his parents and older sister in a rural area. He attends a local public school. His teachers have noted his exceptional memory, particularly in science. However, Oliver's parents and teachers have also observed behaviours and challenges that raise concerns about anxiety and possibly autism. These include:

- **Difficulty with social interaction:** Oliver struggles with social interactions. He does not often initiate play with peers and seems to prefer playing alone. He tends to repeat certain phrases from his favourite science shows during conversations, which confuses other children. His repetitive speech might be a self-soothing practice related to anxiety, or it could be echolalia, a feature often seen in autism.
- **Resistance to change:** Oliver becomes extremely upset with changes in routine, such as a substitute teacher or a rescheduled music class, more so than his peers. His parents notice that he asks repeatedly about schedules and becomes anxious if any usual activities are altered. His heightened distress during changes could be interpreted as anxiety about the unexpected, or it could be a need for sameness and predictability, a common trait in autism.
- **Sensory sensitivities:** He is particularly sensitive to loud noises and bright lights, often covering his ears and getting visibly distressed during school assemblies or birthday parties.
- **Social withdrawal:** Both children with anxiety and those with autism might withdraw socially. For Oliver, it's unclear

whether his avoidance is due to fear of social judgement (anxiety) or difficulty in understanding social cues (autism).

Parental intervention and professional support

Oliver's parents consult with a multidisciplinary team including a GP who refers them to a paediatrician, a psychologist and a speech therapist. This team conducts a thorough assessment, including observation, parent interviews and direct interaction with Oliver.

The school psychologist also evaluates Oliver's behaviour in structured and unstructured settings to observe his social interactions, adaptability to changes and response to sensory stimuli.

The team works closely with Oliver's family to gather a detailed history of his development and behaviours at home and in other settings.

After a detailed assessment, Oliver is diagnosed with autism (ASD – level 2), which accounts for his sensory sensitivities, need for predictability and social communication difficulties. His anxiety is seen as both a part of and a response to his autism, particularly in social situations and when facing sensory overload.

Oliver's intervention plan includes:

- **Behavioural therapy:** Applied behaviour analysis (ABA) to help with social skills and to manage disruptive behaviours.
- **Speech therapy:** Focused on improving his pragmatic language skills.
- **Occupational therapy:** To help Oliver cope with sensory sensitivities.
- **CBT:** Adapted to account for Oliver's autism and to address anxiety, particularly around changes in routine and unexpected events.

- **Family support and education:** Providing his parents with strategies to manage anxiety at home and understand autism.

With targeted interventions and consistent support, Oliver begins to show improvements in handling transitions at school and participates more in activities with his peers. His anxiety decreases as he learns to manage his responses to sensory stimuli and social interactions.

This scenario underscores the complexities of diagnosing and treating children with symptoms of both anxiety and autism. It highlights the importance of careful, comprehensive assessments to understand the interplay between different conditions and tailor interventions that address all aspects of a child's development.

Are disorders being over-diagnosed?

There has been a huge spike in the number of families seeking help for anxiety in their child or teenager. Similarly, there has been a large increase in presentations of families seeking an ADHD or autism diagnosis. I believe that we are in a 'catch-up phase', as these issues may have flown under the radar in the past and were not recognised. It's unclear whether Covid-19 lockdowns made the symptoms of anxiety and other disorders more obvious within households, or families are simply feeling less stigma attached to seeking help.

The impact of our Western lifestyles also cannot be ignored. The environmental influences discussed in this book – such as the use of social media and screens, stress and being busy, inability to be bored and wind down, poor sleep and diet – are also linked to the prevalence of mental health difficulties in children. There is emerging evidence that our exposure to plastics and pollution, and certain medications during pregnancy, may also increase the risk that a child will develop an anxiety disorder.

I am convinced more than ever that the emergence of screens from a very young age is a key driving force in how our children view the world. Screens should be viewed with caution, as most of our children and teens simply don't know how to handle them. It is up to us as adults to provide screentime boundaries and be aware of what children are viewing. This is not to say screens are completely terrible. They have given us a window into the world like nothing else before, and provide educational opportunities along with communication at a much faster rate. How we handle that is still being determined. It is obvious though that the more a child indulges in using their favourite gaming machine, the more their mental health will be impacted.[16]

From my observations in working with families, it can be a difficult habit to break. Children with anxiety and ADHD tend to be more attracted to screen use as a way of managing their symptoms. Screens can have a calming effect on them. So in reducing or stopping screens, there needs to be alternative activities that continue to engage them. Children and parents could brainstorm what these might be. Ideas include an activity after school (such as taekwondo or gymnastics), incorporating family board games, puzzles, or going for a walk to the park or beach. These can all provide positive feelings similar to watching screens and provide a distraction to reduce that temptation.

PART II
MANAGING ANXIETY

CHAPTER 4

Creating a Secure Base

It is the parent's role to create a secure attachment base with their child.

As I mentioned in the introduction to this book, a child who has a secure attachment base with at least one person in their life who provides them with a loving bond is better able to cope with stress. Loving, responsive and stable relationships with caring adults are essential for healthy social and emotional development in children. Secure attachment to the primary caregiver in the early years helps to protect against anxiety and boosts the child's ability to cope with stress.[17]

Just like establishing trust, children need to know they are safe. Their home base needs to be secure for them. This does not refer to having security cameras around the outside and locks on the doors (although this is important in some parts of the world). Instead, a safe base with children represents protection physically and emotionally through your behaviour and communication. This means demonstrating love through physical contact, such as hugging and kissing your child and reminding them that they are safe with you. Creating a secure base for a young child might mean sitting next to their bed as they drift off to sleep.

As children grow older, they become more confident and their needs change – but they still require a secure base. As a parent, be there for your child when they need it. This does not mean giving them 100 per cent of your attention at all times. If your child needs you all the time, they might have separation anxiety; but otherwise, explain that you will, for example, sit with them for the next 30 minutes to play. After this period, you might need to complete your own tasks before coming back to see what they are doing. We cannot be with our children 100 per cent of the time, nor should we feel guilty for not doing this.

According to Circle of Security International, for a secure base, children need their parents to:

- Protect and comfort them
- Delight in them
- Help them organise their feelings
- Support their exploration
- Watch over them
- Help them
- Enjoy being with them
- Be bigger, stronger, wiser and kind
- Follow their need whenever possible
- Take charge whenever necessary.[18]

I would add to this: love abundantly.

The most important thing of all is to be loved and cared about. This gives children a sense of security, belonging and support. Love is free, but it can take time to develop and doesn't come easily for some of us. Some of us were raised by less loving parents ourselves and struggle to show what love is. We don't necessarily need to hug or kiss to show our children love. Love equals time. Being present and showing an interest in your child is what creates a loving bond. Taking your child out for a special outing is as caring as sitting with them and listening to them read. Give them undivided attention, put your feelings aside and try to understand what they are telling you. Aim to be present for those crucial moments, and above all, tell them you love them.

A child stands at the centre of their circle with parents nearby in their inner circle. From here a child has outer layers of their circle that they might explore such as nature, food, school and new activities. Children should be encouraged to explore these 'circles' and discover new things, but have the comfort to return when they are ready.

Building resilience

Resilience is the ability to adapt to and overcome adversity or difficult situations. Children who have a secure attachment base are more likely to be resilient. Humans are not 'born resilient' – it is a trait that is developed and strengthened over time.

A child who builds skills to develop resilience is less likely to have anxiety. Of course, this is a generalisation, as there are children who may seem resilient but still develop anxiety disorders. Remember when we talked about the causes of anxiety? Some children might be more impacted by their genetics than by their environment. It is impossible to predict this. There is no genetic test for anxiety like there is for other conditions.

There are four key aspects to building a child's resilience:

- Foster positive relationships through a supportive environment
- Encourage problem-solving skills
- Allow failure and celebrate the wins
- Support emotional regulation and allow children to name how they feel.

Allowing children to take risks is a crucial component to building resilience. Depending on their age, children should be allowed space to explore the world around them. If they do fall or injure themselves, this also builds resilience. Once they are feeling better they can try again. Then, when they succeed in a particular task they feel good about this and will continue to explore new challenges.

As you let go of your child at the playground and allow them to explore, watch their cues. It's a bit like a rubber band: finding the right amount of tension in the band will allow them distance without letting the band break. Avoid being overprotective, but also keep them safe.

Children like having a sense of independence, and I believe that we can provide this despite our world being perceived as a scary place. We, as parents, need to let go of some of our fears for the sake of our kids. We naturally hold our own anxieties about our environment because we live and breathe it and see so many terrible things happening in our world. I see many parents who were raised in a strict manner, or who have their own anxiety or OCD symptoms related to going outside the house, struggling with this. This is difficult.

We must remain confident that our children can do things for themselves without severe consequences and that we can still be good parents by allowing them to do so. Through empathy, patience, and informed support, we can pave the way for brighter tomorrows.

Working with your child's temperament

Unlike resilience, temperament is more of an inbuilt part of a child's personality. Some children are calm, quiet and passive while others are the complete opposite! We all display different temperaments and this is part of what makes us unique.

Understanding a child's temperament may help you predict their ability to cope with stress. Children who are sensitive tend to be overwhelmed more easily. This is not a bad thing of course as children with a sensitive nature are also very kind, caring and loving. Children who are strong-willed, outgoing, boisterous and loud might brush off stress and not be affected in the same way. This is not to say louder children are not loving and caring, or sensitive children cannot overcome stress, it is just that the way they perceive and react to certain triggers may be different. Both personality types are equally valid and will help to shape their life goals, their careers and ultimately their purpose.

Parents who have a different temperament to their child often find it hard to relate to them, and this can cause arguments or clashes at home. If this is the case for you, it means going on a journey of self-discovery as a parent. Opposite temperaments can work well together but need to compromise. A child who is outgoing, busy and always needing stimulation paired with a parent who is quiet, calm and likes routine can be one example of where compromise is needed. You will learn so much about yourself in raising a child, and not only this, but you will change as a person as your child teaches you about yourself and how you react to the world. As much as a child might need support, we as adults also need support in developing our coping strategies for stress.

While temperament is inbuilt, it can still be moulded over time. A young child may be shy and quiet but develop into an outgoing and confident teen. This is also the case for us as adults. We can learn to accept that routines do change unexpectedly and try not to sweat the small stuff in life. Calming our own stress takes a lot of time. Understanding our own responses to situations also takes time, but it is worth it.

Working with your child's temperament means tuning in to what your child's individual needs are and adapting accordingly. I've only just realised that my seven-year-old doesn't like hugs; she likes high fives. She is not a touchy-feely person, but she loves wrestles and tickles. My nine-year-old, however, won't go to sleep without being tucked in and given a kiss and hug. I am like my nine-year-old, but I've had to adapt the way I communicate and express myself with my seven-year-old to ensure that we don't clash. I've learnt that if I do try to hug her before bedtime, it can lead to her being annoyed. It is amazing how different two children in one family can be and how we as adults must adapt.

How to talk to children about anxiety

A big part of creating a secure base for your child is, of course, talking with them. This is a key way to help them process their emotions and work through any difficulties they are experiencing – including anxiety.

Talking about anxiety with a young person requires sensitivity and understanding. Every child's response to the conversation may be different. Be patient and let them know that you are there to support them through any challenges they may face with anxiety. Building trust and open communication will help create a safe space for them to share their feelings and seek help if needed.

Even for healthcare professionals, describing terms such as anxiety, depression, mental health and feelings to children, and asking them to reflect on these, can be a challenge. There are age-appropriate ways to do this so that the child understands where you are coming from.

Normalise emotions

Normalising can be very empowering. It helps children realise they are not alone. Everyone goes through mental health difficulties at some point in their life. Children are not excluded from this. There are some good books (listed in the Resources section at the back of the book) that will help you talk to your child about anxiety and emotions in a way that is easier for them to understand. Try not to be judgemental or act surprised with what you might hear from them. Thank your child for sharing the information and let them know you are always there for them if they need to talk about it again.

You may have experienced the same situation as your child and can tell a story of your own experience with worry and fear and how it affected you. In general practice, I'll often talk about the fact we all have big feelings from time to time. I'll use case examples such as a child I've seen who's scared to go on a sleepover, or another child who struggles with doing new things. Parents should still centre the child in the discussion even though they may be sharing their own experience.

Use simple terms

I try to avoid the term 'anxiety' as much as possible when I'm talking to young people, partly because I don't want a child to feel there is anything wrong with them. There is nothing wrong with them; their mind is just taking over how they feel, and we need to figure out what the driving forces are.

I might say something like: 'What is your level of worry in this situation between zero and 10? Has it ever been 10 out of 10? We sometimes call this a panic attack. What has helped this number go down to, say, three or four?'

Or: 'What is your greatest fear? Do thoughts ever go around and around in your head, and you don't know how to stop them or let them go? Do you ever feel like a volcano, where the pressure builds up until it explodes into an anger meltdown?'

Children often smile when they hear these questions as many have experienced these feelings and can resonate with what I am asking them. This helps them to feel less alone or judged and gives them a starting point for the conversation.

Other questions I ask are very open-ended: 'Tell me about a time you felt worried, sad or mad. What led to that event? Did you manage to work through it, or did you need support?'

I might also ask:

- 'How often do you feel worried or nervous on a typical day?'
- 'On a scale of one to 10, how intense are your feelings of anxiety during challenging situations such as tests, presentations or social events?'
- 'Do you notice any physical symptoms when you're anxious, such as a racing heart, sweating or stomach discomfort?'
- 'Are there specific triggers or situations that tend to make your anxiety worse?'
- 'How do you usually cope with your anxiety? Are there any strategies that you find helpful in reducing your feelings of unease?'

Talk when the time is right

Rather than asking how a child feels in the middle of a meltdown, speak to them when they are in a calmer state of mind. This might be when you're driving them to school, when they aren't looking directly at your face. Children can be less threatened in this situation and may be able to open up more. For example, you could say: 'I noticed you were having a hard day yesterday after school. You were really cross with your brother. Where did that come from?'

Later in the book we'll talk through some examples of ways to speak to children about specific behaviours and manifestations of their anxiety.

Be open and honest with your child

Having an open and honest relationship with your child is something we all strive for.

The balancing act is working out what we should tell our child and what should be kept to the adults. My go-to when I don't want my child overhearing something is to spell it out, but unfortunately, this doesn't work after the age of about six!

Children are often very good at listening to adult conversations. Too often my children have pulled me up on something I was talking to my wife about when I didn't realise they were listening. This just goes to show: you need to keep adult conversations away from the dinner table and the central family area. They should be had after the children are in bed.

In terms of balancing honesty with oversharing, think about whether the information is relevant to the child or appropriate for them to hear. Are you discussing an event from a long time ago that really has no bearing on today? Perhaps a car accident you had in your 20's that left you shaken? Yes, this is a good teaching point about being careful in the car, but how relevant is it that your child is aware of this event? Be mindful of oversharing, particularly if your child is struggling with anxiety.

Also consider whether the information is going to cause harm. For example, if you give them information about local bushfires, might this actually provoke an emotional response that is difficult to calm down? If you are talking about war in another country, does your child need to know details of the death toll? If they are learning about it at school, perhaps, but otherwise, is it needed or appropriate?

Ensure your voice and demeanour are calm when you are talking about anxiety or big topics such as serious world events. Be selective and focus on the positive aspects such as how lucky we are in our country and what we have in our own home that makes us fortunate.

Why is a secure base so important?

If all of this seems like a lot of work, you're right. It *is* a lot of work! It might take us our entire parenting life to figure it out. Know that it is worth it.

After 50 years of research, we know that the more secure children are, the more they are able to:

- Enjoy more happiness with their parents
- Feel less anger at their parents
- Turn to their parents for help when in trouble
- Solve problems on their own
- Get along better with friends
- Have lasting friendships
- Solve problems with friends
- Have better relationships with siblings
- Have higher self-esteem
- Know that most problems will have an answer
- Trust that good things will come their way
- Trust the people they love
- Know how to be kind to those around them.

Every ounce of energy you invest in your child is worth it.

Making time for you

If you're feeling overwhelmed as you read this, remember it's important to look after your own wellbeing as well as that of your children. Part of this is to make time for yourself. It feels like we never have time, but we do. Everything can wait: the dishes, the washing, the cooking. It won't go anywhere. What you can't wait for is your own mental wellbeing. If you have support available, make use of it. Too many times have I met couples who have offers of meals and babysitting from grandparents, but they don't use them.

It can be very difficult dealing with an anxious child. Manage your own reactions, and do some things for yourself. Run a hot bath, read a book when your children go to bed, talk to a friend about how you're feeling, go for a walk. Remember the basics: eat well, sleep well and exercise. Give yourself permission to take time off. You can't be helpful to your child if you don't take care of yourself.

You also need to be careful not to pass your own fears on to your children. Try to present a neutral reaction to situations and let your child know it's safe to explore their feelings.

CHAPTER 5

Practical Ways to Help Your Child

If you have noticed anxiety in your child you are most likely wondering how best to help them cope and move forwards. The good news is that most anxiety-related problems in children and teens can be managed without medication. It might take some time to figure out, but a combination approach works well.

First, find a good GP who listens to what the key areas of concern are. Check if a referral to a psychologist or mental-health-trained occupational therapist (OT) might be helpful. At the same time, you can work through the exercises and ideas provided in this chapter to find what helps to relieve your child's suffering.

Resetting an overly sensitive nervous system

Resetting an oversensitive nervous system can be challenging. However, with patience and care, it is possible to unwind and reset. It is difficult because for children with anxiety, it can become the 'new norm'. They are in a constant state of flight or fight which is not sustainable because it uses up so much energy and interferes with their life in so many ways. For the child, it might be hard to remember what it was like to feel calm and 'normal'. So for some children it will take a good routine of self care with proper sleep, nutrition, mindfulness, encouragement to take on new challenges and eventually succeed at them, regular psychological support and a lot of patience. In time, the nervous system will respond and become less stressed.

We often get caught up in trying to achieve too much in life and forget how busy we are and how this is affecting our children.

Many families find success in adopting a slower pace of life, particularly in terms of after-school activities. During school holidays, the absence of these commitments can provide a welcome relief from anxiety.

A lot of life's extracurricular activities can wait. Stick with the basics for now and gradually build from there. Good sleep, three meals a day (pick your battles when it comes to the quality of that food), reduced screen time, getting to school and basic social interactions with family and friends.

It's important, however, not to replace activities with excessive screen time. Instead, encourage quieter moments at home or in nature with friends. Consider removing one or two activities that your child finds less enjoyable. Even a brief respite from these commitments may have a positive impact.

Some families find it easier to stop all the unnecessary activities and, when the time is right, slowly reintroduce them. Other families have a screen 'detox' for a few weeks. Allowing a child to be bored and live without screens is an excellent way to manage the frequent nagging and fixation some children have for screen time. It does make it hard for parents, though, as you are the one who has to deal with the consequences of this!

As part of the slowing-down process, I suggest allocating a time where you are 'present' with your child. This might be the first thing you do each day. Spend whatever time you have available – even 10, 20 or 30 minutes of quality time. Children crave quality time with their parents and it is these short bursts that can help towards this. Ask your child, 'What would you like to do?' Play with them, sit with them, read to them, draw with them, jump on the trampoline, go for a walk to the park, go out for a chino – it doesn't really matter what the activity is, just be present with no distractions, phones or chores. I used to think quality time meant taking my kids on outings to the zoo, aquarium and beach. While these are fun and definitely great family time, it is often the simplest activities that help a child feel valued.

Let your child know how long you have to spend with them, and that once this time is up they can carry on with what you had started or play something else by themselves. You can also pre-warn children that you have certain tasks you need to complete that day.

If your child really struggles with boredom, create a list together of fun things they like to do at home. Put the list on the fridge so that they can refer to this for ideas. I sometimes pull out two or three puzzles and games or set up an activity for them such as Lego, craft or a project they need to complete. The best part about boredom is the ability for it to spark creativity. Some of my children's best artwork has come from having nothing to do!

In resetting your child's sensitive nervous system it's also important to monitor your own anxiety levels, as anxiety can be contagious. When our children are anxious, it's easy to become anxious ourselves. Modelling good coping mechanisms and remaining calm can help your children regulate their emotions. Some children need physical touch, while others require space, so be mindful of their individual needs. In the event of a meltdown, arguing with your child rarely produces positive results. Instead, try to redirect their energy towards a calming activity and allow them time to de-escalate.

Identifying emotional triggers

As your child grows and develops, you will start to figure out what most commonly triggers their big emotions. Some common scenarios that parents tell me lead to anxiety in their children include:

- Turning off screens
- Large gaps between eating
- Not enough sleep
- Being told 'no'
- Change (including change of routine)
- New situations
- Friendship issues
- New environments
- Relief teachers.

Triggers to anxiety and distress in children can be wide and varied. What might affect one child won't necessarily affect another. Just being aware of triggers through common patterns of behaviour, and working on those, can be a good first step. For example, where routine changes are a trigger, have days off routines, such as in the holidays and on weekends. Allow children to be more flexible with time and practise this approach by not becoming stressed yourself when you're running late to school or an appointment.

Mindfulness and relaxation techniques

Mindfulness is a powerful tool for people of all ages to manage their emotions and stress levels. It's all about being present in the moment and fully aware of your thoughts, feelings and surroundings. By practising mindfulness, children can learn to manage their emotions and feel more in control of their health and wellbeing.

Apps such as Smiling Mind, Headspace and Calm are a great place to start when introducing mindfulness to your child. All provide short and easy-to-follow mindfulness exercises for children.

When explaining mindfulness to a child, it's important to make it relatable and easy to understand.

Following are some mindfulness and relaxation exercises and explainers for you to try with your child. I suggest encouraging children to practise mindfulness techniques for 10 minutes a day.

The glitter jar

Ask your child to imagine their mind is like a big jar full of glitter. When they're feeling happy, the glitter settles down, and they can see everything clearly. But sometimes, when they feel upset or worried, the glitter gets all stirred up, and it's hard to see clearly or feel calm.

Tell your child that mindfulness is like magic for the glitter jar. It helps them settle the glitter and makes their mind feel clear and peaceful again. It's about paying attention to how they feel, what they see and what they hear, right in this moment. It's like taking a deep breath and giving the mind a little break from all the busy thoughts.

You can help your child practise mindfulness by encouraging them to do simple things such as taking a few deep breaths, feeling the ground beneath their feet, or listening to the sound of birds chirping. Explain that when they do these things, they're giving their mind a little holiday from all their worries, and that helps them feel better and more focused.

Remember to keep it playful and engaging, using examples and activities that the child can relate to. Mindfulness can be taught through fun exercises such as mindful breathing, mindful eating (eating a small piece of food very slowly and noticing its taste and texture), or even a mindful walk, where they pay attention to the sights and sounds around them while taking slow steps. As with anything new, this method of relaxation takes practice. Many children tell me they tried it but it was 'boring' or 'not helpful'. Mindfulness is like learning to ride a bike. It might take weeks but eventually should become a routine that just happens as part of a daily ritual for the family.

The magical bubble wand

Breathing exercises are a great way to help your child practise mindfulness, and I'll share a few ideas with you in the coming pages.

A simple technique that I've found works wonders is to ask your child to imagine there is a magical bubble wand inside of them. They can use their breath to create a stream of magic that helps dispel any feelings of worry or fear. Following is an example of how I might describe this technique to a younger child:

> *Imagine you have a magic bubble wand inside you. When you're feeling worried or scared, you can blow magical bubble breaths to make those feelings go away!*
>
> *Let's try it together. Take a slow, deep breath in through your nose, and imagine you're blowing up a big, magical bubble inside your belly. Now, hold that breath for a moment, and feel the magic filling you up. And now, gently blow out the breath through your mouth, just like you're blowing bubbles. Watch as the magical bubbles float away, taking away any worries or nervous feelings with them.*
>
> *Remember, whenever you feel anxious or scared, you can use your magic bubble breaths to make yourself feel better. It's like having a little superpower right inside you!*

Belly breathing

Another technique to encourage deep breathing is belly breathing. Start by having the child place their hand on their belly and take a deep breath in through their nose. As they inhale, their hand should rise with their belly.

Then, have them slowly exhale through their mouth and feel their hand fall as their belly deflates. Encourage them to focus on their breath and notice how their body feels as they breathe in and out.

It's a simple exercise, but it can help them feel calmer and more centred.

The five-finger technique

This is an alternative breathing exercise you can try. It involves breathing in slowly while tracing up the edge of one finger, then breathing out slowly while tracing down the other side. Ask your child to follow these steps, illustrated in figure 3:

1. Place the index finger of one hand on the outside of the thumb on your other hand. As you breathe in, trace up to the tip of your thumb, and as you breathe out, trace down the inside of your thumb.

2. On your next inhale, trace up the outside of your index finger, and on the exhale, trace down the inside of your index finger.

3. Inhale and trace up the outside of your middle finger. Exhale and trace down the inside of your middle finger.

4. Keep going until you've traced your entire hand.

5. Reverse the process and trace from your pinkie back to your thumb.

Five-finger breathing is great because it brings several senses together at the same time: you're watching and feeling your fingers while you're paying attention to your breath. This not only requires awareness of multiple senses (seeing and feeling) but an awareness of multiple locations in your body (your two fingers, your two hands and your lungs).

FIGURE 3: THE FIVE-FINGER TECHNIQUE

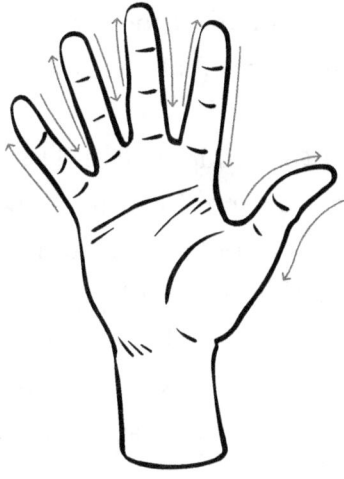

Progressive muscle relaxation

Progressive muscle relaxation is a great technique to teach to or practise alongside your child. Following are the steps to doing so:

1. **EXPLANATION:** Begin by explaining to the child that sometimes our bodies hold onto stress without us even knowing it, and this can make our anxiety feel worse. Tell them that by squeezing and relaxing their muscles, they can help their body feel less tense.

2. **STARTING POSITION:** Have the child find a comfortable position, either sitting or lying down in a quiet space where they won't be disturbed. They can close their eyes

if they feel comfortable doing so, which can help them focus on the exercise.

3. **BREATHING:** Instruct them to take a few deep breaths – inhaling slowly through their nose, holding it for a couple of seconds, and then exhaling slowly through their mouth. This helps to initiate relaxation.

4. **TENSING MUSCLES:** Guide the child to focus on one muscle group at a time. They can start with their feet and move upwards, or begin with their head and work downwards. For younger children, it's often easier to start with their hands. Ask them to make a tight fist with one hand, squeeze as hard as they can (without causing pain) for about five seconds, and notice how the tension feels.

5. **RELAXING MUSCLES:** After tensing each muscle group, they should quickly release it and feel the muscles become loose and limp. Encourage them to pay attention to the sensation of the muscles relaxing and the differences between the tense and relaxed states.

6. **CONTINUE THE PROCESS WITH ALL MUSCLE GROUPS:**
   – Hands and arms (squeeze hands into fists, then relax; bend arms at the elbows tightly, then relax)
   – Shoulders (shrug them up to the ears, hold, then relax)
   – Forehead (raise eyebrows as high as possible, hold, then relax)
   – Eyes (close them tightly, hold, then relax)

- Cheeks and jaw (smile as wide as possible, hold, then relax; then open mouth wide, hold, then relax)
- Stomach (suck it into a tight knot, hold, then relax)
- Legs and feet (point toes upwards to tighten calf muscles, hold, then relax; curl toes downwards, hold, then relax)

7. **CLOSING THE SESSION:** Once they have worked through all the major muscle groups, ask them to spend a minute or two just lying quietly with their eyes closed, breathing deeply and slowly. Encourage them to imagine a peaceful scene or think of something that makes them happy.

8. **REFLECTION:** After the session, talk about what the experience was like. Ask them which parts of the body felt the tensest and which felt the most relaxed. Discuss how they might use this technique whenever they are feeling anxious.

Encourage the child to practise progressive muscle relaxation regularly, ideally daily. The more familiar they become with the technique, the more effectively they will be able to use it to manage anxiety when it arises.

The worry monster

The worry monster is a great metaphor to use with children to help them make sense of and work through their feelings. Following is how I might explain it to a child:

Anxiety is a bit like having a tiny worry monster inside you. This little monster likes to make you feel scared or nervous about things, even if there's nothing to be afraid of. It's like when you're going to a new school or meeting new people, and your tummy feels all fluttery, and your heart beats faster. That's the worry monster saying, 'Be careful, something might go wrong!'

Sometimes, the worry monster gets too loud, and it makes you feel uncomfortable, like when you're afraid of the dark or when you have to do something new for the first time. It's like having lots of big feelings all mixed up together.

But guess what? We can be the boss of the worry monster! We can learn ways to calm it down and feel better. We can talk to someone we trust, like Mum, Dad or a teacher, and they can help us understand our feelings. We can also take deep breaths, just like smelling a flower and blowing out a candle, to show the worry monster that it's okay.

And you know what else? Everyone feels a little worried sometimes – it's normal! But we can practise being brave, like superheroes, and face the worry monster together. It might take time, but we can show the worry monster who's in charge!

A practical strategy in this situation is to ask your child to draw their worry monster. What does it look like? How big is it? What colours does it have? What is it saying?

I have seen some very insightful worry monsters where children draw things they never would have talked about. One example was a worry monster next to a tomb stone. The child explained he was worried his parents were going to die, and he was going to be left alone.

A toolkit for anxiety, separation or sadness

Creating a toolkit for a child to use when they are feeling worried or upset can be a helpful way of empowering them with coping strategies. The toolkit can be a physical box or a metaphorical concept that includes various items or techniques to soothe and calm the child during difficult moments. Here are some things that can be included in the child's toolkit:

- **BREATHING EXERCISE CARDS:** Create or print out cards with simple deep breathing exercises, such as those I described earlier in this chapter. These cards can guide the child through calming breathing techniques even in your absence.
- **COMFORT OBJECTS:** Include a favourite stuffed animal, a soft blanket or a small toy that brings comfort to the child. Holding or hugging these items can help provide a sense of security during moments of distress.
- **WORRY STONE OR FIDGET TOY:** A smooth worry stone or a small fidget toy can be used as a grounding tool to help the child focus their attention and reduce anxiety.
- **STRESS BALL:** A stress ball can be a great tool for releasing tension and anxiety through squeezing.
- **JOURNAL OR DRAWING PAD:** Encourage the child to write

down their feelings or draw their emotions. Expressing their thoughts on paper can be a healthy way of releasing pent-up emotions.

- **FEELINGS CHART:** Create a feelings chart with various emotions depicted through pictures or emojis. The child can point to how they are feeling at the moment, helping them identify and communicate their emotions. Office supply and discount department stores often sell these with magnet faces that your child will stick on depending on how they feel.
- **POSITIVE AFFIRMATIONS:** Create cards with positive affirmations such as 'I am brave', 'I am loved' or 'I can handle this'. Reading these affirmations can help the child feel more confident and reassured.
- **MINDFULNESS ACTIVITIES:** Include simple mindfulness activities such as colouring sheets, a mindfulness book, or one of the apps I have listed in the Resources section at the back of this book. These activities can help the child stay present and centred.
- **CALMING MUSIC OR GUIDED MEDITATION:** Provide headphones and a device with calming music or guided meditations designed for children. Listening to soothing sounds can help the child relax.
- **FAMILY PHOTOS:** Include pictures of loved ones or cherished memories. Looking at these photos can bring feelings of warmth and security.
- **CONTACT INFORMATION CARD:** Include a card with important contact numbers, like parents' or caregivers' phone numbers, or a trusted adult they can talk to when they need support.

— **COPING CARD:** See the 'coping card' I created (figure 4) which can be used in any intense, stressful and overwhelming situations. Try creating your own coping card with your child or teen. It can be very reassuring to know your child has something they can look at when they are going through a difficult period in their life.

FIGURE 4: COPING CARD

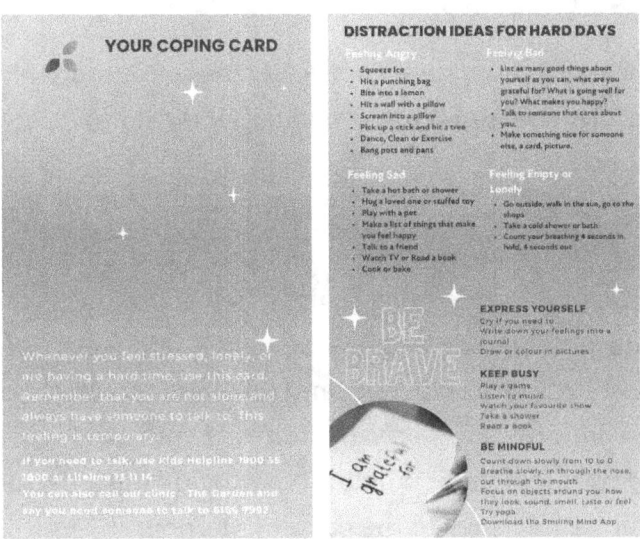

Encourage the child to use their toolkit whenever they feel worried or upset. It's essential to discuss each item with them and explain how it can help during difficult times.

Focus on strengths and success

The optimal approach for enhancing your child's learning and behaviour centres on a strengths-based approach. Rather than only dealing with their weaknesses, it's vital to identify and nurture their interests and particular skills. This approach helps the child to feel empowered and motivated to achieve their goals and celebrate their accomplishments.

Celebrating every small victory, even with assistance, will encourage them to excel. With your unwavering support and motivation, your child can conquer so much more!

Exercise together

Any movement counts as exercise. Encourage outdoor play where possible. Get your child involved in a sport they love, or try a few different ones.

Going for walks can be very calming for a child. Talk about what you see, hear, smell and feel. For example, on a simple walk to the park you might see birds, flowers, plants, leaves, cars, bikes and people. You might smell grass, smoke and fresh air. You might hear birds chirping and the wind blowing. You might feel the wind, the rain, the sunshine on your back, the ground beneath your feet. It is so helpful to provide this grounding and bring your family back to the present moment.

To incorporate exercise into family routines, consider these examples:

- **FAMILY WALKS OR BIKE RIDES:** Take regular family walks or bike rides in your neighbourhood or local parks. This activity allows everyone to enjoy fresh air and engage in light exercise together.
- **OUTDOOR PLAYTIME:** Encourage unstructured outdoor play, such as playing tag, kicking a ball or flying kites.

Outdoor play helps children burn off energy and enhances their creativity.
- **HIKING OR NATURE EXPLORATION:** Plan family hikes or nature walks on weekends to explore nearby trails and natural surroundings. This can be both physically and emotionally rewarding.
- **DANCE PARTIES:** Organise spontaneous dance parties at home where family members can dance to their favourite music and have fun while getting active.
- **SPORTS AND GAMES:** Play sports or active games as a family, such as basketball, soccer, badminton or frisbee. This promotes teamwork and healthy competition.
- **FITNESS CHALLENGES:** Create fun fitness challenges or obstacle courses in the backyard for the whole family to participate in.
- **SWIMMING:** Go swimming together at a local pool or visit the beach if possible. Swimming is an excellent full-body exercise that children often enjoy.
- **YOGA OR STRETCHING:** Practise family yoga or stretching sessions to promote flexibility, relaxation and mindfulness.
- **GARDENING:** Involve children in gardening activities, which can be both physically and emotionally satisfying as they witness the growth of plants they care for.
- **ACTIVE COMMUTING:** Whenever feasible, walk or bike with your child to nearby destinations, such as school or the supermarket, instead of using the car.

Remember that family exercise should be enjoyable and inclusive. Involve children in choosing the activities and be supportive. By making exercise a regular part of family life, you can promote not only physical health but also emotional wellbeing for all family members.

When your child or teenager is ready, they might like to enrol in a team sport. This has even more benefits in developing social skills, physical activity and resilience such as learning what it is like to win and lose, dealing with injury, working with teammates and a coach. Team sports can be a wonderful way to support a child's routine, distract from anxiety and build their confidence.

Active listening

Mums field an average of 288 questions a day from their young children, with the number of questions asked varying by the age of the child. The most enquiries per day come from four-year-old girls – the daily number of questions they put to their mums is an incredible 390![19]

It is impossible to respond to all of those questions. We would never get anything done. It might be easier to allocate specific time to your child for chatting where you put your phone away and actively listen. Good times for this are around the dinner table or in the morning while having breakfast. Children feel important when you listen, so this investment of your time will pay dividends in building their self-esteem.

What's the easiest way to talk to a child? Being physically at their level works well. Many children I see will start off shy and withdrawn when entering the room. Some hide behind their parent. It takes time to establish rapport. I have my biggest wins when I kneel down to the child's level. For this reason, I have purchased a small table and chairs for my consultation room. I can then sit on one side and the child on the other. We colour and draw while we chat. There are a few aspects of this that contribute to its success. I am distracting the child by colouring and drawing. I am showing an interest in their work. I am doing the same thing as them, so they feel validated and listened to. I am at their level, so they feel empowered. Try this at home. In this sort of set-up, I have been able to ask children about their deepest fears. I have established that they might not feel safe in certain environments or that they worry their parents are going to die.

Building self-esteem

> *'To be yourself in a world that is constantly trying to make you something else is the greatest accomplishment.'*
> — RALPH WALDO EMERSON

> *'You'll never look like the girl in the magazine. Even the girl in the magazine doesn't look like the girl in the magazine.'*
> — DANNIELLE MILLER

Our children and teenagers are more self-conscious than ever before. They look at others and think, 'I really want to look like that.' They compare their bodies, personalities and even their wisdom with others. The advent of social media has only encouraged this.

Building self-esteem means allowing our child to determine what is important to them. It also means praising them in a helpful way. It is so easy to praise or reward every effort a child makes. I get caught up doing this with my children or with children I see in the clinic. Whilst we have good intentions in doing this and even feel compelled to do this to encourage them to carry on, we need to be careful with our wording. For example, we might say, 'Your picture looks amazing' or 'This work is so good'. If a child gets used to this level of praise and doesn't get it at some stage, they can feel a sense of failure, especially if we comment when a child's work could be more creative, or they could have achieved more than they did.

This is developmentally normal and not intentional, as parents try to give their child confidence. Try to have various comments in mind that focus on being interested in their actions. Creating positive self-esteem is more about the effort than the outcome. This might involve saying, 'I can see how hard you're trying', or even being curious about their picture, 'Tell me a bit about your picture', 'what led you to that answer?' or 'What else could you add to it?' These statements are not critical of the child. They also do not encourage perfection by helping the child think about what they are doing and knowing it is okay to make a mistake.

Give praise in a way that helps your child grow. Kasey Edwards and Dr Christopher Scanlan discuss this in their book, *Raising Girls Who Like Themselves*. Rather than simply praising the work, take the opportunity to turn the child's question around and direct them back at them. When they ask you, 'Do *you* like my outfit/dance/artwork?', flip the question around and ask, 'Do you like your outfit/dance/artwork?' The child's opinion matters most, not ours, and they should be proud of themself. How does this actually build self-esteem? It teaches them to like themselves for who they are, not for what other people see.

It is important to praise your child for facing their fears. Involve your child in activities that help them feel proud. Find activities that reinforce that they are good at something (sports, music or art, for example). This helps instil a sense of belonging and pride. You can also give your child responsibilities around the house and let them be in charge of something at home, such as making sure the dog gets a walk every day, putting out the bins, making beds or learning to make their own breakfast.

Parenting programs

The most commonly recommended parenting programs in Australia are the Positive Parenting Program (Triple P) and the Circle of Security. Both tend to run locally in various community groups such as schools at low cost or for free. Most psychology groups and OTs offer family therapy. Likewise, most local councils offer programs for families, some at low cost.

Working with different behaviours

Following are some basic tips for working with both positive and challenging behaviours:

- Catch your child behaving well and completing tasks correctly, and give them specific praise – for example, 'Great packing away', 'Good listening', 'Nice job on sitting still' or 'Thank you for helping'. Remember your child may not be able to repeat these successes in new situations, so ongoing teaching, support and patience is required.
- Ignore minor negative behaviours whenever possible, so your child doesn't receive attention as a reward.

- Then, when your child starts behaving positively, it's important to give them immediate attention.
- If your child is misbehaving, it's important to interrupt them immediately, grab their attention and redirect them to another activity to prevent further escalation.
- If they continue to behave inappropriately, specifically label their unacceptable behaviour – for example, 'no hitting', instead of making broad negative statements such as 'Stop being naughty.' Follow this with a clear, calm instruction about what you want them to do instead – for example, 'Put your hands down/use a quiet voice/sit still.'
- Don't argue or renegotiate consequences. It's best to be consistent, especially across both parents.
- Consequences should be relevant, proportional and consistent.
- Identify a range of reinforcements/rewards that work best with your child. The greater the variety of rewards, the better.

Collaborate with your child's school

Collaboration with school staff can be essential in supporting children with anxiety disorders at school. School-based interventions can include modifications in the classroom environment or strategies to reduce academic and social stressors.

Stepladder approach

For fears and phobias such as going to school or going out of the house, you can try a stepladder approach yourself at home. It is a good way to de-escalate a child's fight-or-flight response in different situations. You do this by breaking down worries into manageable chunks and gradually working towards a goal.

Let's say your child is afraid of water and swimming. Instead of avoiding the pool, create some mini goals to build their confidence. Start out by just sitting and watching other kids swimming. As they feel more comfortable, get them to try dangling their legs in the water, then standing in the shallow end, and so on.

Inspire your children to be superheroes

Kids love superheroes. Why is this? Superheroes promote fantastic imagination and show kids they can achieve anything if they put their mind to it. Superheroes have an extraordinary power or ability to face their enemies. We need to inspire our children to become their own superheroes – to take on their fears and fight through them. For children who are bullied, this is a great example of how we really want them to imagine themselves.

Think about who you look up to for inspiration. What is it about that person that you find inspiring? In the same way that you look up to those role models, your children look up to you.

Don't forget to have fun!

Having fun as a family can really transform how everyone is coping. It is common sense to have fun as a family, but we often forget to prioritise it. We become so caught up in our busy week that we lose sight of what the whole purpose of life really is. It is okay to be silly, to tickle your children, to laugh with them, to laugh at them, to tip them upside down, to give them 'blurters' and to let them climb all over you. Teaching your children to have fun makes them feel a valued member of your family.

Special outings and rituals can provide your family with a sense of unity. You can spend a lot of money on trying to have fun, but you don't need to. I recently discovered that one of the funniest activities my children enjoy is a 'tickle attack'. This comes out of the blue, and when they least expect it, but it certainly provides those big belly laughs that release endorphins. A day building forts out of furniture is equally as powerful as a day spending lots of money at a carnival – quite often, even more so. I urge you to keep it simple. Here are some questions you can ask yourself:

- Do you have a family ritual?
- Do you go away as a family?
- Do you share happy experiences and laugh together?
- What makes your children laugh?
- When was the last time you helped them do this?

Having fun also needs to incorporate sensory play. Allowing your child to be messy and dirty is an essential part of their development and reduces their chances of developing sensory-related anxiety.

Let them hang upside down on monkey bars and spin uncontrollably. Yes, it might mean they hurt themselves from time to time. We have progressed too far in the way of being clean and hygienic. This is partly why peanut allergy is rising. At the park, beach or home, let them play, give them a chance to touch different textures. Build a mud kitchen. Take their shoes off. This helps with both proprioception and posture. Most importantly, this freedom teaches children that germs are okay, we can get a bit messy sometimes, and the slimy, gooey feeling of this is simply incredible.

You can also find out about local programs for children. Many regions offer social skills programs, Parkrun for social connection and exercise and group programs for building resilience.

CHAPTER 6

Navigating Challenging Behaviours

This chapter delves into the challenges of managing challenging behaviours at home and school. This is a common struggle for many families I see in my practice. It's not unusual for children to exhibit extreme behaviours, such as screaming or yelling when they don't get their way or becoming aggressive, hitting and punching their parents. Tantrums over minor frustrations and fights between siblings can test the patience and harmony of any household, sometimes leading to prolonged periods of tension and discord.

While these behaviours can be overwhelming, it's important to remember that they are often a part of a child's journey towards emotional maturity. As they grow older, most children gradually learn to manage their intense emotions, offering some hope for families dealing with these challenges.

It's also important to remember that we, as parents and caregivers, experience big emotions, too. A tough day at work or sheer exhaustion can make it harder to handle our children's outbursts calmly. Their testing behaviour can push us to our limits when we're vulnerable. If you tend to respond with anger or become overly reactive, try to have your own strategy for self-regulation and calming down to avoid escalating the situation. Techniques might include taking a few deep breaths, stepping away briefly or engaging in a calming activity.

Modelling these self-regulation techniques for our children and later reflecting on the incident with them can teach valuable lessons in emotional intelligence. By apologising and discussing the difficulties openly, we demonstrate how to handle big emotions constructively. This helps us manage challenging behaviours more effectively and equips our children with the tools they need to navigate their own emotional landscapes.

Tantrums and meltdowns

A tantrum usually has a communicative function, which often involves yelling and screaming. All parents will be tested by this, and it is only natural to feel compelled to yell back. Children are very good at finding a way to hit our nerves and trigger our own emotional response. It can be extremely challenging to do the opposite to this, but it's so important to try. It will take practise and consistency, and the good news is we don't always have to get it right.

It can help to keep in mind that your child might be trying to 'tell' you, via their behaviour, that they are frustrated, scared, tried, hungry, unwell or want attention. They might be communicating that they want something – such as a treat or a toy – or want to avoid something – such as a task or situation they don't like or find challenging.

A meltdown, in contrast to a tantrum, does not have a communicative purpose. Rather, it is the child's response to feeling completely overwhelmed by environmental stressors.

One benchmark many parents use is that a tantrum is likely to subside if no one is paying attention to it. This is opposed to a meltdown, during which a child loses control so completely that the behaviour only stops when they wear themselves out and/or the parent is able to calm them down.

Regardless of whether you're looking at a tantrum or a meltdown, always try to meet your child's challenging behaviours with patience and empathy. Then, figure out what works for your child specifically so you can help them through it.

Helping your child through meltdowns

Dealing with a child who is experiencing a meltdown can be challenging. However, by following the following tips and being patient, you can help your child through any meltdown they may experience.

In order to make the situation easier for both you and your child, there are a few things to keep in mind. First, stay calm and speak in a low, soothing voice. Becoming upset or angry yourself may only exacerbate the situation for your child.

Remember that, during a meltdown, your child may not be able to articulate what is wrong. It's best to focus on helping them calm down before trying to discuss the issue.

Unlike tantrums, meltdowns are unlikely to resolve on their own. Identifying and addressing the triggers can help prevent future meltdowns.

Reducing sensory input can be an effective way to begin the de-escalation process. Even if overstimulation is not the sole cause of the meltdown, it's a good place to start. Here are some ways to do this:

- 'Divert the energy' by distracting your child with something completely different – for example, going outside is a very good way to help a child regulate.
- Dim bright lighting.
- Turn off music.
- Move away from crowded, noisy areas.
- Provide earmuffs or noise-cancelling headphones to block out any background noise that can't be reduced or eliminated, such as traffic sounds.
- Move away from strong odours.

Once the stressors that led to the meltdown are removed or reduced, some children benefit from having a trusted person stay close by as a comforting presence, while other children prefer being given space to regulate themselves. Providing a low-sensory, comfortable space to sit for some 'quiet time' can be helpful. A familiar spot is ideal if possible.

Some children may react strongly to physical touch while in a meltdown state, as they are already overloaded, and this gives them one more thing they must process. For some children this can include touch that is intended to be comforting, such as hugs. Therefore, it may be useful to ask your child first if they want a hug before giving one.

Check in to see if your child is actually hungry. Food can make a big difference to how a child feels.

After your child has calmed down, ask if they know what triggered the meltdown. This shows them that you care about their feelings and want to understand their perspective. Then, share your own thoughts on what might have caused the outburst to help your child gain insight into their emotional responses.

Take note of any triggers and early warning signs that you observed during the meltdown. Keeping a record of what worked and what didn't work can be helpful for future reference. Then, share this information with other adults who care for your child. Burnout and fatigue can contribute to meltdowns, so it's essential to maintain open communication.

At the end of the day, many children are at high risk of experiencing meltdowns, especially if their day involved lots of social interactions and sensory input. Consider scheduling time for your child to unwind and decompress before moving on to their evening routines. This can help them regulate their emotions and avoid meltdowns.

CASE STUDY

MIA'S SUPERMARKET MELTDOWN   Age: 3

Background

Mia is generally a cheerful and energetic toddler who enjoys playing with her toys and interacting with family members. However, like many children her age, she sometimes has difficulty managing her emotions, especially when she is tired or overwhelmed.

On a particular day, Mia has been out running errands with her mother all morning and it's approaching her usual naptime. She is now in a busy supermarket with her mother.

As they pass the confectionary aisle, Mia points at a brightly coloured packet of M&M's and asks her mum if she can have it. Her mum, knowing Mia has already had a treat earlier and also mindful of her impending naptime, says no.

Tantrum unfolds

- **Initial reaction:** Mia's face crumples and she begins to cry loudly, attracting the attention of other shoppers.
- **Escalation:** When her mother tries to move the shopping trolley along, Mia throws herself on the floor, kicking her legs and screaming. She refuses to get up, saying repeatedly, 'I want those chocolates!'
- **Peak:** The tantrum intensifies as Mia throws nearby lightweight items off the shelf in frustration. Her cries become more intense, and she begins to sob uncontrollably.

Parental intervention

- **Calm and collected:** Mia's mother knows that talking too much or showing her own frustration can sometimes escalate Mia's emotions further. She stays calm, lowers herself to Mia's eye level, and speaks in a gentle but firm voice.

- **Validation and redirection:** She acknowledges Mia's feelings by saying, 'I can see you're really upset because you want the M&M's. It's hard to not get what we want.' Recognising that Mia is tired and likely overwhelmed, she gently but firmly suggests, 'Let's go pick out a storybook to read after your nap.'
- **Follow-through:** Mia's mother offers her hand to help her up, reminding her calmly that they will be heading to the car now. She tries to remain calm, helping Mia transition her focus from the chocolate to the promise of a story after her nap. After a few more sniffles, Mia allows her mother to pick her up. She continues to whimper a bit but starts to calm down as her mother talks about what they'll do when they get home, shifting her attention away from the tantrum.

This example illustrates a typical tantrum in a young child triggered by denial of a desire, compounded by fatigue. The mother's response highlights effective strategies for handling tantrums: maintaining calm, validating the child's emotions, offering alternatives and redirecting the child's attention to upcoming positive activities.

These tactics help defuse the situation and support the child's emotional regulation skills.

Rage

If your child is in a rage, screaming and hitting you, or hitting their siblings, it is almost impossible to allow this to continue without intervening. Children with anxiety do present with physical and at times aggressive symptoms like this. But children *without* anxiety can also present like this purely because they are tired or didn't get what they wanted. So how do we manage this? Keeping it consistent, regardless of the cause and across all parents or caregivers in the house, is a good first step.

A child who is hitting requires some boundaries. Meet them eye to eye, remain firm in your voice without screaming or yelling and tell them, 'You can feel angry, but you cannot hurt me or your sibling.'

Children who are dysregulated simply cannot rationalise in that moment and will need to be separated from the trigger. This might mean spending time in their room to allow the feeling to settle. This doesn't mean time out, more of a de-escalation. Going outside is another option; whatever helps to divert the energy somewhere else, away from the trigger.

Your safety and the safety of your other children is very important, so if a child is very aggressive, they may need to be physically contained by picking them up, removing anything dangerous and separating them until they calm down.

When the moment has passed, you will need to debrief on what exactly happened. This might be on the way to school the next day, in bed that night or even a few days later. Ask your child what leads them to feeling so upset and if there's anything you can do to help.

If your child doesn't know, you can make suggestions. 'I saw you feeling really angry the other day. You ended up hitting your brother. I can see that you must have felt very frustrated, maybe because he took your toy, or I put the iPad away? Was this what happened?'

From there you can progress to solutions that are practical and fair. Let them know that next time they feel themselves getting angry enough to want to hit or hurt someone, they should go to their room or go outside and allow that angry feeling to settle down. You might create a toolkit that they can use including things such as squeezy toys, a punching bag, a trampoline or a weighted animal toy that is ready for when they have excess negative energy that needs to be released.

Food-related anxiety

Food can be a real trigger of strong emotions for children. This is often linked to a sensory-related problem that leads your child to struggle with different textures, not just related to food.

I see many children who are selective when it comes to food. They are fussy with flavours and may have a restrictive diet as a result. This works both ways: anxiety itself can cause a child to not feel hungry. They might be struggling at school with keeping up, making friends, or experiencing separation anxiety and as a result have reduced appetite.

It can be really challenging to develop a balanced diet in a child with anxiety. Quite often anxiety alone can limit a child's interest in food, but also the variety of foods. Many children with anxiety struggle with sensory processing, meaning they don't like strong tastes or flavours.

This can be incredibly stressful for parents and caregivers. The more you push, the harder it gets. Do your best and continue offering variety, but without getting too caught up in the emotion of it all. This is easier said than done.

Accept that your child might genuinely have difficulty with swallowing certain types of textures, and that no amount of bribery, pressure or anger will change this, for now. I have noticed a gradual improvement in acceptance of food groups from the middle to upper primary school age groups. This means generally children will improve with very little intervention.

Tastebuds evolve over our lifetime. Infants have around 30,000 tastebuds; by adulthood, only about a third of these remain. So, when children eat they are tasting food with higher intensity and flavour than adults.

Children are also hardwired to find calories to support their growth and weight. One sugary flavour they seek is abundant in breastmilk – which is potentially why they often prefer 'white' foods versus colourful foods. Some children can reject bitter foods and see them as 'poison'. The reason many children don't eat their greens may be that the bitter flavours are being amplified by so many tastebuds. By the time their palates are ready and more accepting of vegetable flavours, they may be negatively associated with bad memories – such as being told they must eat them or being punished for not eating them.[20]

I see a significant number of parents with stress purely around food. Whether it be that their child 'never eats what's on their plate' or 'overeats junk food' or 'will only eat a selection of three different dinners on rotation', I can empathise with how this affects families. Parents are left with pressure to ensure their child grows, while their child becomes frustrated by ongoing pressure to eat. It creates a storm, but it doesn't need to be like this.

One of my favourite sayings to parents going through this is 'pick your battles'! Some battles are just too big and should be avoided.

Let's take a look at some strategies to help children thrive even when they won't eat what you ask them to.

You provide, they decide

This strategy is appropriately named 'the division of responsibility'.[21] Your job is to choose and prepare the food, provide regular mealtimes and snacks and make eating times pleasant and calm. Your child's job is to eat the amount they need, choose what they eat from your offerings and learn to behave well at mealtimes. Buffet style mealtimes work well where the food is laid out and each person can choose what they are going to put on their plate.

It is also helpful to offer children their preferred foods regularly rather than trying to make them eat new foods too often. Give them a daily mixture of foods they know and love and small amounts of 'test foods' that they are still learning to accept. Be patient! Usually somewhere between age six and 10 children (and perhaps their parents) become more relaxed with food and are willing to be more adventurous.

Eat together

Families tend to be getting busier and more diverse in their activities. This can lead to segregated mealtimes where not everyone is available to eat together. Eating together provides a pause to the day and creates positive feelings around food. Family mealtimes may not be possible every night, but at least creating a ritual like this every so often enables these positive interactions to occur.

When eating together, turn off screens (no phones or television). Traditional face-to-face interaction becomes so important in our busy world and helps your child to feel valued.

Fill in the gaps

Some fussy eaters may need extra nutrition. An oral nutritional supplement can be used in this instance to fill in the gaps, especially when a child is too busy, too tired or distracted to eat a solid meal. Using an oral nutritional supplement also provides reassurance that they are getting some added nutrients that they may otherwise have missed out on.[22]

If in doubt request an appointment with your GP or paediatrician to arrange a thorough review such as measuring the child's BMI and blood testing for specific nutritional deficiencies. Parents are often surprised that their child is still growing adequately despite the perceived lack of nutrients. Despite this, I do tend to refer to a dietitian to look at what else can be done to include replacement of specific vitamins that might be lacking. For example, it is common to find a child's iron is low and requires additional supplementation.

Here are some other ideas that might help with food-related anxiety:

- **AVOID EXCESSIVE SUGAR AND CAFFEINE:** Minimise the intake of sugary foods and beverages, as well as caffeinated drinks. High sugar consumption and excess caffeine can lead to energy spikes and crashes, which might worsen feelings of anxiety.
- **INCLUDE COMPLEX CARBOHYDRATES:** Choose complex carbohydrates such as whole grains (brown rice, quinoa,

whole wheat) instead of refined carbohydrates (white bread, sugary cereals). Complex carbs can help regulate serotonin levels, which can promote a calmer mood.
- **PRIORITISE HYDRATION:** Ensure your child stays well hydrated throughout the day. Dehydration can lead to irritability and difficulty concentrating, which may worsen anxiety symptoms. It can also cause problems like constipation which can further impact a child's mood.
- **KEEP VITAMINS AND MINERALS IN MIND:** Certain vitamins and minerals can play a role in supporting the nervous system. Encourage the consumption of foods rich in B-vitamins (leafy greens, legumes and eggs), magnesium (spinach, nuts and seeds) and zinc (oysters, beef and pumpkin seeds).
- **LIMIT PROCESSED FOODS:** Minimise the intake of processed and junk foods, which may contain additives and preservatives that could affect mood and behaviour.
- **AVOID THE 'HANGRY' CHILD:** Have food ready for school pick-up. This is commonly a time a child will be on edge as they haven't eaten for quite a while, and they will be tired!
- **INVOLVE YOUR CHILD:** Whenever possible, involve your child in meal planning and preparation. This can help them feel empowered and may increase their willingness to try new, healthier foods.

Bedtime and sleep anxiety

It can be common and quite normal for children to develop anxiety at bedtime. This peaks anywhere from four months of age through to around eight years of age.

Sleep anxiety can be related to the difficulties children have in separating from their loved one, or fear of the dark and related themes such as ghosts and monsters. There has been a significant increase in sleep-related problems In adolescents stemming from the use of devices in bed.

For children who are struggling to break the cycle of sleeping in their parents' bed or spending significant periods of time trying to fall asleep (more than 30 minutes), the following practical solutions may be helpful:

- **CONSISTENT SLEEP SCHEDULE:** Set a regular bedtime and wake-up time for your child, even on weekends. Consistency helps regulate their internal clock, making it easier to fall asleep and wake up.
- **BEDTIME ROUTINE:** Create a calming bedtime routine that lasts about 20 to 30 minutes. Activities such as reading a book, playing with Lego, doing a puzzle, playing a card game, taking a warm bath or listening to soft music can signal the body that it's time to wind down and prepare for sleep.
- **LIMIT SCREEN TIME BEFORE BED:** Screens turn off the body's natural production of melatonin. Even when a screen claims to have options to reduce 'blue light', there is no real evidence that this improves sleep quality. All screens should be turned off at least one hour before bedtime. Exceptions might be on school holidays or for family movie nights on the weekend. Children and teenagers should also avoid using screens in bed. This can be modelled by adults in the family as well so that everyone has the same approach.

- **CREATE A RELAXING SLEEP ENVIRONMENT:** Make sure your child's bedroom is conducive to sleep. Keep the room dark, quiet and at a comfortable temperature. A night-light can provide a sense of security for young children who may be afraid of the dark. A teddy bear or other comfort item can also help.
- **BE MINDFUL OF FOOD CHOICES:** Some foods can disrupt sleep, while others may promote relaxation. Avoid giving your child caffeinated or sugary drinks or snacks close to bedtime. These can make it harder for them to fall asleep, Consider including sleep-supportive foods in their diet, such as bananas, cherries, oats or warm milk.
- **ENCOURAGE PHYSICAL ACTIVITY DURING THE DAY:** Regular physical activity during the day can help promote better sleep. However, avoid intense exercise close to bedtime, as it may make it harder for them to wind down.
- **MONITOR DAYTIME NAPS:** While napping is essential for young children, make sure that daytime naps are not too long or too close to bedtime. Naps that are too late in the day can interfere with night-time sleep.
- **ADDRESS BEDTIME FEARS:** If your child has bedtime fears or worries, take the time to talk with them and address their concerns. Offer reassurance and create a sense of security.
- **TEACH RELAXATION TECHNIQUES:** Teach your child relaxation techniques, such as deep breathing or progressive muscle relaxation, to help them unwind and ease any anxiety or restlessness before sleep (see chapter 5 for more details). There are some good apps for this as well (listed in the Resources section at the back of

the book). Try a gentle foot massage for your child before bed, or a weighted blanket.
- **AVOID STRESSFUL ACTIVITIES BEFORE BED:** Avoid engaging in stimulating or stressful activities or conversations close to bedtime. Encourage calm activities that help transition from active play to relaxation. Avoid reading scary books to your child before bed. Keep your voice calm and soft.
- **LEAD BY EXAMPLE:** Be a role model for healthy sleep habits. Show your child the importance of following a consistent sleep schedule and practising good sleep hygiene yourself.
- **ELIMINATE THE NIGHT-TIME BOTTLE AT AN APPROPRIATE AGE:** After around 12 months of age, the routine of using bottles to fall asleep can be more difficult to break. Bottles also affect jaw structure and put your child at risk of dental decay. Show your child that the bottle is now worn out and no longer needed for this part of the day. Children can have a cup of warm milk or Milo if it helps with transitioning away from this habit.

The Royal Children's Hospital has some tips on bedtime routines for children on its website: www.rch.org.au/kidsinfo/fact_sheets/Bedtime_problems

'Camping out'

Are you stuck sleeping in the same bed as your child? Try this clever 'camping out' technique to gradually separate yourselves from each other. Don't expect an overnight fix. The idea is to very slowly desensitise your child to the separation stress and anxiety that occurs when you are leaving them at night-time.

Children can quite naturally fear that being left alone puts them in some form of danger, so again, lots of reassurance is required that you aren't far away and will be there if they need you.

Here are the steps I suggest taking:

- Sleep next to them on a mattress on the floor, all night. Continue for two to three nights.
- Lie with them while they fall asleep, then return to your own bed. Continue for two to three nights.
- Sit on a chair next to them while they fall asleep, then return to your own bed. Continue for two to three nights.
- Move to a room nearby while your child falls asleep, then on to being in the kitchen or doing something nearby where they can hear you. And so on.

For camping out to be successful, it usually takes three to four weeks. If a child decides you being there is a good opportunity to play, remind them that it is sleep time. If this doesn't work, leave the room for a minute or two and return when they are ready to settle down again.

Social media and screens

In my work as a GP I have noticed a concerning trend around the use of social media and screens, particularly for pre-teens and teenagers. I have concluded that there are 'positive' and 'negative' outcomes that can be attributed to the emergence of social media in young people's lives. Social media allows regular social interaction which, for some, is a protective factor when they might otherwise feel lonely or isolated. It is a safety net when they feel troubled by difficult thoughts. They almost always have someone to chat to on one of the dozens of apps they are signed up to. This is the new normal when it comes to social connections and it's often how young people also catch up outside their schools.

On the flip side, social media is surely one reason behind rising rates of adolescent mental health challenges. There is a constant need and desire to be 'better', as there will always be someone that is better on social media. Social media encourages people to post photos of themselves that display their best attributes. This might increase their confidence and build their status in their peer groups, but can also be detrimental to those who feel they are not part of that group or will never be 'good enough'. I can see how this would increase their anxiety as they try to fit in.

I also hear from teenagers being bullied by their peers on social media. This means even when they are not at school the bullying never stops. Rather than being able to switch off and focus on home life, they are switched on 24/7 to the conversations that are occurring among anyone they connect to within their lives. How parents regulate this is a constant stress and challenge.

A study of 563 young adults in the US found that more time spent on social media was significantly associated with anxiety symptoms.[23] The authors hypothesised that social media platforms may be a source of stress contributing to elevated anxiety symptoms and related impairment among users. However, it was also noted that individuals with anxiety may engage in more frequent social media use as a form of validation to enhance their self-worth. So, while there is a strong relationship between anxiety disorders and social media use, the study suggests that the association may be complex and not solely causal.

More research is needed to understand the effects of excess screen time on child development. There are definitely positive aspects to using screens including hand-eye coordination and faster learning and language development, especially through educational apps such as Reading Eggs. The negative effects might be that children find it harder to be bored when they don't have a screen. Screens cause a release of dopamine in the brain, and children then seek this out more often. Boredom is good for children; it sparks their creativity. When they come to you saying they are bored, don't feel guilty!

CASE STUDY

ALEX'S DIGITAL DILEMMA   Age: 11

Background

Alex is in Year 6. He lives with his parents and younger sister.

He has always had an interest in video games and digital media, which his parents initially saw as a harmless hobby. However, over the past year, his parents have noticed a significant increase in the time he spends on his devices.

Alex's screen time has escalated to the point where he spends most of his free time either playing video games, watching videos or interacting on social media. This has begun to affect other areas of his life.

Alex rarely goes outside anymore, even refusing invitations to play with school friends. His physical activity levels have dropped significantly.

Previously outgoing and sociable, Alex now spends lunch breaks at school alone, often on his phone or gaming device.

Alex shows signs of anxiety, particularly when faced with social situations or when asked to disconnect from his devices. He becomes irritable and sometimes panics at the thought of not being able to check his device.

Whenever he feels stressed or upset, Alex turns to his devices to zone out. Gaming can be very calming for him and helps him to deal with his emotions. Requests to stop using screens often lead to arguments and outbursts. Alex struggles to comply with time limits set by his parents, leading to frequent conflicts.

Parental intervention and professional support

- **Setting clear boundaries:** Alex's parents implement a

structured daily routine involving specific times for screen use, including no devices during meals or an hour before bedtime.

- **Encouraging alternative activities:** They enrol Alex in a local soccer club and a coding workshop that meets in person, encouraging interests that are both social and partially related to his interests in technology. He will also attend a Dungeons and Dragons club in the school holidays.
- **Creating a family media plan:** The family works together to create a media plan that includes designated family activities with no screens allowed, such as board game nights and weekend outings.
- **Professional guidance:** Seeing little improvement, Alex's parents seek the help of a child psychologist who specialises in digital addiction. The psychologist works with Alex to address his anxiety, using techniques such as CBT to help him develop healthier coping mechanisms.
- **Parental modelling:** Alex's parents also make a conscious effort to model appropriate screen use, including limiting their own time on phones and computers, especially in the evenings.

Over several months, Alex begins to show improvement. He becomes more engaged in soccer and enjoys the coding club, which allows him to use his interest in technology constructively. Although he still enjoys his screen time, he is better able to disconnect when asked and starts to have fewer anxiety symptoms. His social interactions increase, and he begins to re-establish some old friendships.

How much screen time should my child be having?

Screen time is very individual to different children. Some children cope well with screens, others don't. You will get to know what works for your child and how to manage that. In general, though, it is best to have time limits on screens so that it doesn't become too excessive.

Younger children under two should have very limited screen time. For children two to five it is recommended they have up to one hour of screen time per day (including TV, tablets, phones and computers).[24] Above this age it is very much dependant on what is acceptable for you and your family. There is no magic figure. The right amount of screen time can depend on a range of factors like your child's age and maturity, the kind of content they are consuming, their learning needs and your family routine.

Screens can be a useful mechanism when a child is dysregulated or needs to have some time out and relax. Generally, less stimulating screen activities are more helpful, such as television shows. Keep simulation games such as console and PC gaming on time limits and set an alarm clock that is visible or known to your child.

Give your child a five-minute warning before screens are going off. You will notice that the longer a child uses a screen, the more difficult their behaviour can be when it is stopped.

As discussed earlier, it's best to avoid screens at least one hour before bed. It reduces the melatonin in your child's body which affects their ability to sleep.

Try to role model yourself how you'd like your child to interact with screens. Teach them safety on social media apps by navigating the app together with your child.

It can be easy to focus only on the clock, but the quality and nature of what they are doing online, and your involvement, are just as important. There are also several types of screens. Your child may be using an iPad or computer for school-based learning. This, along with watching a movie or TV show, are less stimulating than using a gaming machine which gives off faster signals and more rapid stimulation.

Computer games are a strong drawcard for children due to the increased release of dopamine that occurs in the brain when they play or interact with them. Dopamine creates a sense of feeling positive and energised. It also leads to substantial levels of concentration and focus. Some children find this difficult to break from, and the draw of this enjoyment is powerful. This is also why children will sit playing games for what feels like hours in one place. In theory, it sounds reasonable that they are feeling calm and happy. This is what we want for our children. The negative of this is that the alternative options, such as studying, reading, going outside or seeing friends, become far less attractive as they may lead to different levels of joy. Striking a balance is crucial for children, and it requires adults to set boundaries to avoid overuse of screens. Another challenge is that a sudden drop in dopamine when stopping a game can be very uncomfortable for a child and lead to strong emotions, arguments, and challenges at home. This is becoming a common issue in many households.

Set clear boundaries through discussion and negotiation for all family members and make this the expectation. An example might be a 30-minute block of screen use before and after school, 60 minutes each day on the weekend, and only commencing on completion of their tasks. This is age-dependent as younger children should have less than older children. Set a timer on a device that alerts the child 10 minutes from the end of their time limit. To reduce the dopamine 'come down' effect, ask them to go outside once they finish. Something is soothing about fresh air and being outside. They could move on to other activities like monkey bars, trampoline, using a bike or gymnastics mat, or playing with a pet. Be firm, fair and consistent. Avoid starting new rules mid-game, such as allowing additional time because they 'are in the middle of something'. This can create confusion and make future attempts less successful. It is usually easier to let your child know about this before the system commences and ask them to check they can save where they get to on the particular game they are using.

Many parents I work with often find it beneficial to 'lower their bar of expectations' when it comes to setting tasks before screen time. Keeping these tasks relatively simple and achievable can help reduce stress and conflict. For instance, younger children could be asked to unpack their school bag, empty their lunch box, and put it in the dishwasher. In the morning, they could make or pack their lunch, get dressed, and have breakfast. Older children could have an additional task, such as doing their homework. By writing out this routine and leaving it on the fridge, parents can provide a clear and consistent guide for their children, making it easier to enforce these tasks before screen time.

Consider your child's screen use in the context of their overall health and wellbeing. For example, is online time getting in the way of their sleep and exercise? Is it impacting their face-to-face connections with family and friends? The answers to these questions will guide you and help strike the right balance of online and offline activities for your child.

The Queensland Government has a good resource on screen time available at: https://earlychildhood.qld.gov.au/earlyYears/Documents/pts-screen-time-and-children.pdf

Additional screen time tips

Some other tips you might find useful are below:

- **SET CLEAR LIMITS:** Establish clear and reasonable screen time limits for your child based on their age and developmental stage. Communicate these limits to them and enforce them consistently.
- **CREATE A SCREEN TIME SCHEDULE:** Designate specific times during the day when screen time is allowed. For example, you can have designated hours for homework, leisure and family activities.
- **LEAD BY EXAMPLE:** Be a positive role model by managing your own screen time. Demonstrate healthy habits by limiting your own device usage, especially during family time.
- **USE PARENTAL CONTROLS:** Utilise parental control features on devices and apps to restrict access to inappropriate content and set time limits automatically.
- **DESIGNATE SCREEN-FREE ZONES:** Establish certain areas in the home, such as the dining room or bedrooms, as screen-free zones to promote family interactions and better sleep quality.
- **ENCOURAGE OUTDOOR ACTIVITIES BEFORE SCREEN USE:** Encourage your child to engage in outdoor activities, sports, hobbies or creative playtime to reduce their reliance on screens.
- **PROMOTE ALTERNATIVE ACTIVITIES:** Provide alternative activities and toys that can engage your child's imagination and creativity without screens, such as puzzles, books, arts and crafts, or board games.

- **USE SCREEN TIME AS A REWARD:** Consider using screen time as a reward for completing tasks or achieving specific goals. This can incentivise positive behaviour and responsibilities.
- **ENCOURAGE SOCIAL INTERACTIONS:** Support face-to-face interactions with family and friends. Plan playdates, family outings and bonding activities to foster real-life connections.
- **WATCH CONTENT TOGETHER:** When your child is watching TV shows or videos, try to watch with them. This way, you can monitor the content and engage in discussions afterwards.
- **USE SCREEN TIME FOR EDUCATIONAL PURPOSES:** Encourage the use of screens for educational purposes, such as interactive learning apps or educational videos.
- **USE APPS AND DEVICES TO MONITOR SCREEN TIME:** Consider using apps or built-in device features that track screen time and provide usage reports. This can help both parents and children become more aware of their screen time habits.

PART III
TREATING ANXIETY

CHAPTER 7

Choosing a GP

When it comes to dealing with important issues such as anxiety and mental health, your first point of call might be your GP. It is so important that you find the right GP: someone who listens and is able to support you with the difficulties your family is experiencing. The process of finding the right GP is not easy. Regardless, your GP should be the centre of your care team and start the process of involving others who might be helpful for your child or teenager's anxiety. I believe your GP is one of your most important allies when managing a child with anxiety. They need to be part of your journey, to navigate between allied health professionals such as physiotherapists and specialists and ensure everything has been checked and everyone is talking to each other. The best approach is a team approach and your GP should coordinate that team.

We now live in a world where knowledge is everywhere, and where many parenting or health questions can be answered within a few seconds online.

In my experience, it is not unusual for a parent to come in and open their consult by saying, 'Now, you're going to think I'm silly, but ...' as a I wait in anticipation for the 'silly problem' they may have just researched on Google to find a really tricky, unusual diagnosis or treatment. My answer to that is, 'There is nothing I haven't seen'! Of course, in reality there is nothing too silly either. We all go through periods where we think, 'Gosh, my child's problem could be really serious', or we second-guess ourselves and our judgement. This is natural, especially when surrounded by information from a wide range of sources that may or may not be accurate, including parents' Facebook chat groups.

Finding a GP can be a bit of a challenge. GPs are quite booked up, and some also charge a gap because of the rising costs involved in running a medical practice. There's the basics such as looking for one close by, finding a kid-friendly clinic, considering fees, availability before and after school and the look and feel of the clinic. You might also want to take note of things like, do the receptionists give you a friendly smile? Is there space for breastfeeding?

Be prepared for your appointments

You may have a GP or paediatrician who has less experience in managing mental health in children and needs some guidance or support in order to help you. They might refer to a specialised clinic or get you to come back when they have more information. To be as prepared as possible, I suggest completing the following checklist and bringing it to your appointment to help your GP understand your child's history and concerns.

Child's school information

School name:

Year level:

Teacher:

Close friends:

Attendance rate:
- ○ Regular (90–100%)
- ○ Moderate (70–89%)
- ○ Low (below 70%)

Favourite subject (select all that apply):
- ○ Maths
- ○ English
- ○ Arts
- ○ Science
- ○ Music
- ○ Sports
- ○ HAAS (Humanities and Social Sciences)

Least favourite subject (select all that apply):
- ○ Maths
- ○ English
- ○ Arts
- ○ Science
- ○ Music
- ○ Sports
- ○ HAAS (Humanities and Social Sciences)

Average grades:
- ○ Excellent (A)
- ○ Good (B)
- ○ Satisfactory (C)
- ○ Needs Improvement (D)
- ○ Failing (F)

Feedback from the teacher:

Learning and school concerns

Parents' concerns about learning:

Previous schools:

After-school activities/sports/commitments (select all that apply):
- ○ Sports
- ○ Music lessons
- ○ Art classes
- ○ Other: _____
- ○ Scouts/Girl Guides
- ○ Tutoring
- ○ None

Home life and activities

Home activities and hobbies (select all that apply):
- ○ Playing outside
- ○ Reading
- ○ Playing with toys
- ○ Other: _____
- ○ Watching TV
- ○ Video games
- ○ Crafting

Screen time (hours/day):
- ○ Less than 1 hour
- ○ 1–2 hours
- ○ 2–3 hours
- ○ More than 3 hours

Types of screens used (select all that apply):
- ○ TV
- ○ Tablet
- ○ Smartphone
- ○ Computer
- ○ Gaming console

Family information

Siblings and family (circle all that apply):

○ No siblings   ○ 2+ siblings
○ 1 sibling   ○ Extended family living together

Parental separation:

○ Yes   ○ No

Family history of anxiety:

○ Yes   ○ No

○ Court orders (if applicable): _____

Behaviours and emotions

Describe behaviours and emotions:

Anxiety score at home (circle one):

0 1 2 3 4 5 6 7 8 9 10

Anxiety score at school (circle one):

0 1 2 3 4 5 6 7 8 9 10

What makes anxiety better?:

What makes anxiety worse?:

Specific anxieties or fears (select all that apply):

○ Sounds   ○ Textures
○ Tastes
○ Other: _____

Treating Anxiety | 139

Sleep patterns

Sleep duration:

○ Less than 6 hours   ○ 8–10 hours
○ 6–8 hours   ○ More than 10 hours

Time to fall asleep:

○ Immediately   ○ 30–60 minutes
○ 15–30 minutes   ○ More than 60 minutes

Sleeps in own bed or parents' bed:

○ Own bed   ○ Both
○ Parents' bed

Quality of sleep (select all that apply):

○ Snoring   ○ Nightmares
○ Restless legs   ○ Sleep walking
○ Grinding teeth   ○ Ends up in parents' bed
○ Bedwetting

Wake up time:

Energy level on waking:

○ Very energetic   ○ Low energy
○ Moderate energy   ○ Very tired

Diet and nutrition

Typical breakfast:

Typical lunch:

Typical dinner:

Snacks:

Sugar intake (select all that apply):
- ○ Soft drinks
- ○ Cordial
- ○ Lollies
- ○ Packaged foods

Emotional regulation

Describe emotional regulation (select one):
- ○ Normal for age
- ○ Up and down
- ○ Very dysregulated over small things

Previous treatments for anxiety (select all that apply):
- ○ Medications
- ○ Psychology
- ○ Occupational therapy
- ○ None

Health conditions and medical history

Other health conditions:

Current medications:

Previous surgeries:

Additional concerns

Any other concerns you want the GP to know about?:

___

By providing this detailed information, you will help your GP to better understand your child's needs and plan the most appropriate care and support.

CHAPTER 8
Psychological Treatments

Psychology remains the mainstay of treatment for all childhood anxiety-related problems. Regardless of any other treatments that are implemented, all children who have problematic anxiety should have some form of psychology. Nowadays this is available both face-to-face and online. There are many options and variations of psychology depending on where you live and how easy it is for you to access this treatment.

It's essential to remember that children are unique individuals, and the effectiveness of treatment can vary from child to child. Early intervention and seeking help from a qualified mental health professional – such as a psychologist or occupational therapist (OT) – is always a good first step. Parental support, understanding and involvement in the treatment process can significantly contribute to the child's progress and recovery.

Finding the right psychologist

Finding the right psychologist or OT can take time. As a first step, ask your GP for recommendations of local providers who you can research online and work out who might be a good fit.

From there you will need to consider availability (some have waitlists), whether they work in school hours or outside school hours, and if they offer online or face-to-face service.

You will also have to consider who they are. What is their gender and approximate age, and how might your child relate to these factors? Some children click better with a certain gender and age group. There tends to be greater availability of female psychologists and OTs.

Consider the cost, too. Generally, all private psychologists and OTs will charge a gap payment on top of private health insurance or a mental health treatment plan. (We'll discuss mental health treatment plans in more detail in chapter 9.)

What does a psychologist do when working with children?

Psychological involvement is important for children who have difficulties with anxiety that impacts their school or home life. Psychologists can also help with parenting by giving tips and ideas on how to best respond to the child.

Children will usually need several sessions to establish rapport with the psychologist and undergo therapy. Many children will need this therapy long-term. It is important to discuss the goals of care with both the GP and psychologist to make sure you're getting the most out of these sessions. If you don't feel you are benefiting, be upfront and let your GP or the psychologist know.

Confidentiality rules mean if your child sees a psychologist on their own, the psychologist may not be able to share every detail of what was discussed with you. However, the involvement of family is very important, and you should have the ability to have regular discussions with the psychologist.

Let's take a look at some of the specific psychological treatments you and your child may encounter.

Cognitive behavioural therapy (CBT)

CBT is considered one of the most effective therapies for treating anxiety in children. It helps children identify and challenge negative thought patterns and irrational fears. CBT also teaches coping skills and relaxation techniques to help children manage anxiety more effectively.

CASE STUDY

JAMIE'S JOURNEY THROUGH CBT   Age: 9

Background

Jamie is in Year 3 at a local public primary school. He is generally well-liked by his peers and performs well academically. However, he experiences significant anxiety about speaking in front of the class, a requirement in his current grade level for various presentations and reports. Jamie feels extremely nervous days before he is scheduled to present in class. His anxiety manifests as stomach aches, headaches and sleep disturbances. He becomes so worried that he starts to avoid school on days when presentations are due.

Parental intervention and professional support

Jamie's parents consult with a child psychologist who recommends CBT. The psychologist explains that CBT will help Jamie understand the connections between his thoughts, feelings and behaviours, and teach him strategies to cope with his anxiety.

- **Identifying negative thoughts:** In his sessions, Jamie and his therapist work on identifying the negative thoughts that pop up about speaking in front of the class. For example, Jamie often thinks, 'Everyone will laugh at me' or 'I will forget everything I have to say.'
- **Challenging negative thoughts:** Jamie's therapist teaches him to challenge these thoughts by looking for evidence that contradicts them. The therapist asks, 'Has anyone laughed at you before during presentations?' or 'What usually happens when you speak in front of the class?' Jamie realises that his peers are usually supportive, and he rarely forgets what to say completely.

- **Replacing negative thoughts:** Jamie learns to replace negative thoughts with more realistic and positive ones. Instead of thinking 'Everyone will laugh at me,' he starts to think, 'My friends want me to do well, just like I want them to succeed.'
- **Behavioural experiments:** The therapist introduces Jamie to gradual exposure to his fear. This begins with Jamie practising his presentation in front of a mirror, then presenting to a small group of family members, and gradually building up to presenting in front of a small group of classmates.
- **Learning relaxation techniques:** Jamie learns several relaxation techniques, such as deep breathing and progressive muscle relaxation, which help reduce his physical symptoms of anxiety before and during presentations. He learns to take a big five-second breath in, hold it for two to three seconds, then a big five-second breath out, a minute or two before his presentation.

Over several weeks, Jamie's confidence grows. He starts to feel less anxious about presentations and even volunteers to go first in his next class presentation. His physical symptoms of anxiety diminish significantly, and he no longer feels the need to avoid school on presentation days.

This example demonstrates the core components of CBT – cognitive restructuring and behavioural interventions – and how they can be applied to a specific case of anxiety in a child. It highlights the therapy's practical application and its effectiveness in helping children cope with anxiety in a structured, supportive way.

Exposure therapy

Exposure therapy is commonly used for treating specific phobias and social anxiety in children. It involves gradual exposure to the feared situation or object in a controlled and supportive environment, helping children overcome their fears.

Parental involvement and family therapy

Involving parents in the treatment process can be highly beneficial for children with anxiety disorders. Family therapy can help improve communication, reduce family stress and provide support for the child's treatment.

Play therapy

Play therapy is a therapeutic approach used with younger children to help them express their feelings and emotions through play. Play therapists use toys, games and other creative activities to engage children and address their anxieties.

Social skills training

Social skills training can be beneficial for children with social anxiety. This therapy helps children develop appropriate social skills and build confidence in social situations. Some psychology clinics offer group-based therapy to help with social skills.

There are a number of social skills groups in Australia to help support a child's resilience and confidence. Consider Scouts and Girl Guides, Parkrun, local kids' gyms, Standing Strong, dance and sport clubs, OT or psychology group programs, local council programs and university-led programs.

CHAPTER 9

Treatment Plans

Dealing with child mental health challenges can be a stressful and isolating experience. It's important to remember that you are not alone and building a support team to share the responsibility is crucial. There are always people you can talk to for support and help.

In this chapter, we will discuss mental health treatment plans as an effective way to engage with professionals such as psychologists, occupational therapists (OTs) and social workers. When you need a referral to a psychologist or another specialist, a mental health treatment plan is a comprehensive way to start.

What is a mental health treatment plan?

A mental health treatment plan is a structured and coordinated plan detailing the support and treatment for individuals experiencing mental health challenges. It is a formalised document, usually prepared by a GP, that outlines the person's needs and goals, and the services and treatments they will access to address their mental health concerns. Mental health treatment plans are commonly used to access subsidised mental health services under the Australian healthcare system.

A mental health treatment plan provides more detail than a standard referral. It outlines the specific needs and goals for your child's mental health care. This detailed approach ensures that the psychologist or specialist clearly understands your child's situation and can provide targeted support.

Medicare requires that there is a mental health diagnosis to be eligible for a mental health treatment plan.

Anxiety is considered a 'symptom' and technically not a diagnosis. You may find that your GP lists an 'anxiety disorder' on the plan in order to meet this criteria. If it is not clear what the diagnosis is (which often it isn't in children), there are other options the GP can use. It is best to discuss this with them.

Here's how a mental health treatment plan works:

- **INITIATING THE PROCESS:** If your child or teen is experiencing mental health difficulties, the first step is to reach out to your primary care provider, which could be your GP or a psychologist. They will assess your child's mental health and discuss your concerns.
- **CREATING THE PLAN:** If the healthcare professional determines that your child would benefit from additional support, your GP will complete a mental health treatment plan. This plan will outline your child's mental health goals, and the treatments and services they need. The mental health treatment plan allows you to access specific types of mental health services at a subsidised cost. The plan may include sessions with psychologists,

a social worker or a mental-health-trained occupational therapist.

- **NUMBER OF SESSIONS:** The plan typically provides Medicare rebates for a specific number of sessions per calendar year. The number of sessions may vary depending on your needs and the type of mental health treatment plan you have. The most common plan is for an initial six sessions followed by a review with the GP to open up a further four sessions.
- **REVIEW AND ADJUSTMENTS:** The mental health treatment plan is not a fixed document. It can be reviewed and adjusted based on your child's progress and changing needs. If necessary, your healthcare provider can make changes to the plan to better address your child's mental health challenges.
- **REFERRALS:** If your child requires services beyond the scope of their primary mental health treatment plan, your GP can refer you to other specialised mental health services such as a child psychiatrist, child development service, child and adolescent mental health service or other not-for-profit organisations.

Setting goals and moving forward

One of the key components of a mental health treatment plan is the inclusion of specific goals. These goals help to provide direction and focus for the treatment process. It can be easy to get caught up in the emotions and stress of dealing with mental health challenges, but having clear goals can help you stay focused on the positive outcomes you are working towards.

Benefits of a mental health treatment plan:

- **COMPREHENSIVE ASSESSMENT:** A thorough evaluation of your child's mental health needs.
- **TARGETED SUPPORT:** Ensures that the psychologist or specialist understands your child's specific needs.
- **MEDICARE REBATES:** Potential financial support for treatment if a diagnosable condition is present.
- **GOAL SETTING:** Helps to keep the focus on positive outcomes and progress.

Building your support team

Engaging with a psychologist or other specialist through a mental health treatment plan is a significant step towards building a supportive team around your child. This team can include:

- **GPS:** Provide ongoing medical support and referrals.
- **PSYCHOLOGISTS:** Offer specialised mental health care.
- **OCCUPATIONAL THERAPISTS (OTS):** Assist with sensory and motor skill development.
- **SOCIAL WORKERS:** Provide social and emotional support for the family.

A mental health treatment plan is a valuable tool for addressing your child's mental health challenges. By working with your GP to create this plan, you can ensure that your child receives the comprehensive support they need.

What is a chronic disease management plan or care plan?

A care plan can coexist with a mental health treatment plan. Care plans can be useful if you need to incorporate additional providers, such as an exercise physiologist, speech therapist, or occupational therapist.

A child is eligible for a care plan if they have a chronic condition (a diagnosed condition including a mental health condition) lasting longer or expected to last longer than six months. This provides annual funding towards the cost of up to five sessions. It rarely covers the entire amount of the sessions, and gap payments with private providers may be applicable.

To be eligible to access this funding on a care plan for allied health professionals (OT, psychologist, physiotherapist, exercise physiotherapist, dietician), there needs to be three providers involved in the care of the child. Generally this would be the GP, a specialist and the allied health provider.

What is the National Disability Insurance Scheme (NDIS)?

The NDIS does not fund services for childhood anxiety alone but may be able to support children with comorbid conditions such as autism or another permanent disability or for children who have significantly impaired functional capacity. There is also an early intervention pathway for younger children where a specific diagnosis may not be required. For more information on eligibility requirements review the NDIS website: www.ndis.gov.au.

How do I know if services will be bulk billed?

With a mental health treatment plan, you may be eligible for bulk-billed services, which means the provider accepts the Medicare rebate as full payment, and you won't have any out-of-pocket expenses. In most cases, though, there will be a gap payment, which means you will need to pay the difference between the Medicare rebate and the provider's fee.

Private health insurance may be an alternative source of funding. You can always contact your insurer to ask if funding supports psychology and other mental health services, and what the rebate will be.

Headspace offers bulk-billed psychology with a mental health treatment plan for children aged 12 to 25. Each state in Australia has its own publicly funded service, often known as the Child Development Service (CDS) and Child and Adolescent Mental Health Service (CAMHS). These also offer psychology; however, wait times can be extensive, and there are referral criteria that apply.

If funding is difficult, ring up the clinic you are considering and ask about lower-cost options. Some clinics have psychology registrars who have almost completed their training and can be seen at a lower cost. Some universities also offer a similar service. Psychology registrars do not require a referral from your GP as they do not accept a mental health treatment plan.

The Brave Program is an interactive online program for preventing and treating childhood and adolescent anxiety. The programs are free and provide ways for children and teenagers to better cope with their worries. There are also programs for parents. For more information visit: https://brave4you.psy.uq.edu.au

CHAPTER 10

Medication

In managing anxiety disorders in children and teenagers, most cases can be effectively addressed through non-medical interventions such as therapy, behavioural strategies and supportive measures such as managing sleep, diet and routines. However, in instances where the anxiety is particularly severe or resistant to these approaches, medication can play a crucial role in providing relief and improving quality of life. When children do not respond to the therapies and strategies outlined in this book, introducing medication might be the next logical step. Certain conditions, such as obsessive-compulsive disorder (OCD), have shown significant improvement with the use of medications when appropriately diagnosed and treated.

Typically, a paediatrician or child psychiatrist decides to start medication. These specialists have the expertise to evaluate the need for medication and to prescribe it safely. In some cases, however, a GP with specialised training or additional skills in child mental health may also initiate medication. Regardless of who prescribes it, medications in children require careful monitoring and follow-up to ensure they are effective and to manage any potential side effects.

This chapter will guide you through the considerations, processes and precautions involved in using medication to treat anxiety disorders in children. It aims to give you the knowledge and confidence to understand when medication might be appropriate, how it can help, and the importance of close supervision and regular assessments. Always remember that every child is unique, and this chapter serves as a guide only. It does not replace good medical advice specific for your child.

Antidepressant medication for anxiety disorders

The use of antidepressant medication for children with anxiety disorders is a decision that should be carefully considered and made in collaboration with a qualified mental health professional such as your child's GP, paediatrician or psychiatrist.

Antidepressants can be prescribed for children with anxiety disorders when symptoms are severe, persistent and significantly impact their daily functioning, and when other therapies have been tried and not been fully effective, while the child's mental health continues to decline.

An example of an anti-depressant being prescribed in a child

Let's consider the case of 12-year-old Emily, a bright and talented student who has always excelled in school. Over the past year, Emily's parents and teachers have noticed significant changes in her behaviour. She has become increasingly withdrawn, avoids social interactions, and frequently experiences intense episodes of anxiety, particularly in situations where she has to perform or is evaluated, such as during exams or class presentations.

Despite receiving regular therapy sessions and implementing various behavioural strategies recommended by her psychologist, Emily's anxiety persists. Her condition has started to affect her academic performance, sleep patterns, and overall quality of life. She struggles to complete her homework, has difficulty concentrating, and often experiences panic attacks that leave her feeling exhausted and distressed.

Emily's parents decide to consult with a child psychiatrist after discussing the situation with their GP. During the consultation, the psychiatrist conducts a thorough assessment and diagnoses Emily with generalised anxiety disorder (GAD) and social anxiety disorder (SAD). Given the severity of her symptoms and the limited response to non-medical interventions, the psychiatrist suggests considering medication as an adjunct to her ongoing therapy.

After discussing the potential benefits and risks with Emily and her parents, the psychiatrist prescribes a selective serotonin reuptake inhibitor (SSRI), a type of antidepressant commonly used to treat anxiety disorders in children. The medication is chosen because it has been shown to be effective in reducing anxiety symptoms and improving overall functioning in children with similar conditions.

Emily's treatment plan includes starting with a low dose of the SSRI, with gradual increases to find the optimal therapeutic dose. Regular follow-up appointments are scheduled to monitor Emily's progress, assess for any side effects, and adjust the dosage if necessary. The psychiatrist also coordinates with Emily's psychologist to ensure a comprehensive, integrated approach to her care.

Within a few weeks of starting the medication, Emily's parents and teachers began to notice improvements. Her anxiety episodes became less frequent and less intense, she started participating more in social and academic activities, and her overall mood and energy levels improved. With continued support and regular monitoring, Emily was able to manage her anxiety more effectively, allowing her to thrive both at school and in her personal life.

This example illustrates how, in certain cases where anxiety significantly impairs a child's daily functioning and does not respond to standard therapies, an antidepressant can be a valuable component of a comprehensive treatment plan.

What are SSRIs?

Serotonin reuptake inhibitors (SSRIs) are the most common antidepressant used to treat childhood anxiety. While they are called 'antidepressant', they can be more effective in managing anxiety than depression in younger age groups.

Why are they considered 'off-label' in children and teens?

The Therapeutic Goods Administration (TGA) oversees the approval of specific medication uses in Australia.

The TGA has approved use of SSRIs in Australia for teens 18 years and older, or for OCD in ages 12 to 17. This does not mean SSRIs are not safe or effective in younger children, or that they cannot be used in younger children. The TGA has various reasons for not approving medications; it continues to review the data and information in conjunction with medicine advisory bodies.

There has been a long-term caution in place related to increased suicidal thoughts on initiation of SSRIs in young people. Despite this caution, there is still a lack of good evidence that there is any link between these medications and suicide risk. For more information you can visit the TGA: www.tga.gov.au.

The decision to commence medication needs to be made carefully by weighing up the individual child and their situation, such as the impact of their illness on their life and the risks or side effects of the medication versus the benefits.

Health practitioners will quite often use medications from different classes to treat different conditions and often refer to this as 'off-label use'. This simply means we have experience using the medication and know it works for other conditions as well as what it is approved or indicated for.

Guidelines produced by the Royal Australian and New Zealand College of Psychiatrists recommend psychological therapies, such as CBT and interpersonal therapy (IPT), as the first-line treatment for anxiety or major depressive disorders of all levels of severity in young people. Fluoxetine is recommended by the Royal Australian and New Zealand College of Psychiatrists as second line.

When are SSRIs used?

When a child experiences moderate to severe anxiety and doesn't respond to psychological or other effective interventions, medication can offer a helpful tool to tackle the biochemical component of anxiety. This can make the introduction of therapy less daunting and more advantageous. While medication is often not the first choice for children, it's a viable option when anxiety is so severe that the child is missing school or unable to cope with their symptoms. I've seen some very positive outcomes from prescribing SSRIs in children including turning their life around from school avoidance to normal attendance, enabling them to rebuild their confidence and self-esteem once again.

How does an SSRI work?

Serotonin is one of the many neurotransmitters in the brain that play a crucial role in regulating mood, emotions, and anxiety levels. It helps to stabilise our mood and increase feelings of well-being and happiness. Serotonin also influences other functions such as sleep, digestion and appetite.

How does serotonin work? Imagine the brain as a network of roads and neurotransmitters like serotonin as cars that travel along these roads, carrying messages from one place to another. Think of neurons, or nerve cells, as the intersections or stops along these roads. When a car (serotonin) reaches an intersection, it delivers its message to the nerve cell. The car then needs to travel across a tiny gap called a synapse to reach the next neuron. This process of travelling and delivering messages is crucial for regulating how we feel and behave.

In normal traffic flow (balanced emotions) – a well-functioning brain – the cars (serotonin) move smoothly along the roads, and messages are delivered efficiently at each intersection. This smooth flow represents balanced emotions and a stable mood. For example, serotonin levels are balanced when everything is going well in your child's life, and they feel calm, happy and content.

Now imagine a traffic jam where cars are stuck at intersections and can't move forward. This congestion represents anxiety or stress. When there's a disruption in the serotonin flow – either because there isn't enough serotonin or because it's not being efficiently transmitted – messages don't get delivered properly. This can lead to feelings of anxiety, stress, and mood swings.

Using medication such as SSRIs is like implementing a traffic management system that helps clear the roads and reduce congestion. SSRIs prevent serotonin reuptake, meaning more cars (serotonin) stay on the roads, improving traffic flow. This results in better communication between neurons, helping to reduce anxiety and improve mood.

For example: imagine it's rush hour, and there's heavy traffic everywhere. Cars (serotonin) are stuck at intersections, and the roads are congested. Serotonin is not being delivered to where it needs to go as it is stuck in traffic. Messages aren't being delivered efficiently, leading to a build-up of stress and anxiety. This scenario reflects a situation where your child's brain struggles to manage emotions due to low serotonin levels or poor serotonin transmission.

If the traffic lights in a city are not working correctly – for example they are staying red too long or not coordinating with other lights – this can lead to traffic jams, accidents, and increased frustration in drivers. Similarly, if serotonin levels are low or the serotonin system isn't functioning properly (due to genetic factors, stress or dietary deficiencies, for example), this can lead to disruptions in mood, increased anxiety and other emotional issues.

Now, imagine it's a quiet Sunday morning, and the roads are clear. Cars (serotonin) move smoothly, delivering messages quickly and efficiently at each intersection. This represents a state where serotonin levels are balanced, and your brain effectively manages emotions, leading to feelings of calm and well-being.

Why is serotonin important in anxiety?

In people with anxiety disorders, the balance of serotonin in the brain can be disrupted. Low levels of serotonin are often linked to increased anxiety and mood disorders. By increasing the availability of serotonin, medications can help improve communication between neurons, leading to better regulation of mood and anxiety.

How do medications affect serotonin?

SSRIs are commonly prescribed to treat anxiety. SSRIs block serotonin's reuptake (or reabsorption) into neurons. This means more serotonin is available in the synapse, enhancing its ability to transmit messages effectively. Over time, this increased serotonin activity can help reduce anxiety symptoms and improve mood.

Understanding the benefits and monitoring

While medications can be highly effective, they are not a stand-alone solution and should be used in conjunction with therapy and other strategies. It is also essential to monitor for side effects and regularly consult the prescribing doctor to ensure the medication works as intended.

This highlights the importance of maintaining proper serotonin levels and function, which can be supported through various means such as medication (such as SSRIs, which are akin to fine-tuning the traffic lights), lifestyle changes and proper diet, ensuring that our brain's emotional traffic runs as smoothly and efficiently as possible.

Are SSRIs addictive?

There is no evidence that SSRIs are addictive. If a medication is started and later decided not to be helpful, it needs to be weaned off gradually in consultation with your child's doctor. If a dose is accidentally missed, some children can feel side effects such as nausea, dizziness or higher-than-usual anxiety. Aim to be consistent and remember to give the medication as prescribed. If in doubt, speak to your child's healthcare provider and seek advice early.

Will SSRIs change my child's personality?

There is no evidence of SSRIs changing a child's personality. Most children and teenagers will seem calmer, with gradual and sometimes quite subtle changes over a period of time. You may notice they appear happier to go out more, are more relaxed, have less anxiety around school, and are more confident and less agitated.

What SSRI should we start?

Your healthcare practitioner will determine this based on an analysis of the best fit according to their experience and your child's presenting symptoms and diagnosis.

The most commonly used SSRIs in children and teenagers are fluoxetine, sertraline and escitalopram. These medications have received more global research than others. Fluoxetine is the leader when it comes to evidence of use in children and teenagers. It has the greatest data available and is, therefore, often the first used in treatment.

The decision on which medication and the dose depends on many factors, including the child's age, weight, other health conditions, ability to swallow tablets, and diagnosed condition (including whether there is also neurodiversity involved). Beyond this, a paediatrician or psychiatrist may utilise other types of SSRIs if initial therapies have not worked.

How long until an SSRI starts working?

The full effect of an SSRI can take six weeks, or even longer in some cases. If there is no notable difference after eight to 12 weeks, it is worth discussing with your GP or paediatrician to decide if the dose needs to be increased or if the type of SSRI needs to be changed. Sometimes the effect of SSRIs can manifest earlier. In my own practice, I have seen SSRI benefits appearing as early as two weeks after starting.

What happens if it doesn't work?

Depending on the situation, the dose can be increased or weaned off, or the type of SSRI can be switched.

What are the expected benefits?

- **REDUCTION OF SYMPTOMS:** SSRIs have been shown to be effective in reducing symptoms of anxiety in children and adolescents.
- **IMPROVEMENT IN FUNCTIONING:** By reducing anxiety symptoms, SSRIs can help improve the child's ability to participate in daily activities, attend school regularly and engage in social interactions.
- **ENHANCEMENT OF THERAPY:** SSRIs can complement psychotherapy (such as CBT) and may lead to more robust treatment outcomes when used in combination. They can make it easier for your child to participate in therapy and learn strategies to help their symptoms of anxiety.

For full effect to occur, it is generally considered best to remain on an SSRI for six to 12 months or even longer if required. This is very dependent on the situation and how severe the anxiety is.

What are the potential side effects?

- **GASTROINTESTINAL ISSUES:** Common side effects of SSRIs include nausea (mainly in the first week), stomach upset and changes in appetite. Often these occur early on in the course and will self-resolve.
- **SLEEP DISTURBANCES:** Some children may experience difficulty falling asleep or staying asleep.
- **CHANGES IN MOOD OR BEHAVIOUR:** In some cases, SSRIs may initially lead to temporary changes in mood or behaviour, such as increased restlessness or irritability.
- **SUICIDAL THOUGHTS:** There is a rare risk of increased suicidal thoughts or behaviour, especially during the

initial weeks of starting the medication. This risk is very rare and appears higher in adolescents who are experiencing suicidal thoughts or self-harm thoughts. This is sometimes referred to as a 'black box warning', which is what is applied to SSRI product information in the USA for use in children. This is an important side effect to discuss with your treating health practitioner.

If there is any severe deterioration in mood when starting the SSRI, you should speak to your health practitioner urgently or, if they are unavailable, call the local child mental health service or attend a hospital emergency department.

Other tips for SSRIs

- MONITORING AND FOLLOW-UP: Children on antidepressants require regular monitoring to assess their response to the medication and to watch for any potential side effects.
- IMPORTANCE OF PSYCHOTHERAPY: Medication should be considered as part of a comprehensive treatment approach. Medication is not used in isolation but as an adjunct to other treatments.
- RISK-BENEFIT ANALYSIS: The potential benefits of using SSRIs should be carefully weighed against the possible side effects and risks. In some cases, the severity of the child's anxiety may warrant the use of medication, while in others, non-pharmacological approaches may be sufficient.

Melatonin for sleep-related anxiety

One of the most commonly prescribed medications for sleep-related problems in children is melatonin.

Melatonin is a hormone naturally produced by the body that helps regulate the sleep-wake cycle. While melatonin is generally considered safe for adults when used as directed, its use in children requires more careful consideration due to less available research.

The most-studied form of melatonin medication contains the hormone circadin. This will require a prescription from your GP or paediatrician. Many forms of melatonin medication purchased off-the-shelf or online versions do not contain circadin and may be less effective and have less research backing them.

In recent years, there has been a noticeable increase in the use of melatonin medication in children to aid sleep. Many parents are opting for melatonin 'gummies', often purchasing them in bulk from online sources and overseas, hoping to improve their children's sleep. While melatonin can be effective for some children, it's important to note that the evidence supporting its use in paediatric populations is currently limited.

Parents should exercise caution when considering melatonin for their children. The unregulated purchase of melatonin can pose risks, including incorrect dosing and potential side effects. Instead of self-medicating, parents should consult with their GP. A more evidence-based option, such as Circadin, can be prescribed by a healthcare professional. Circadin is a controlled-release melatonin formulation that can be more safely monitored for the correct dose, side effects, and appropriate length of use.

Before taking medication, parents should also consider non-pharmacological approaches to improve their child's sleep, such as those discussed in chapter 6. Remember to use simple strategies first like establishing a consistent bedtime routine, reducing screen time before bed, and creating a calming sleep environment.

The American Academy of Paediatrics and other paediatric organisations have issued guidelines regarding the use of melatonin in children:

- **FOR SHORT-TERM USE:** Melatonin may be considered for short-term use (typically a few weeks) in children with specific sleep difficulties, such as insomnia or circadian rhythm disorders, under the guidance and supervision of a GP or paediatrician. Some children will end up using melatonin for longer than a few weeks. Discuss the benefits versus risks with your doctor when getting a new prescription.
- **SAFE DOSAGE:** The appropriate dosage of melatonin for children varies based on the child's age, weight and sleep issues. A healthcare professional can determine the right dosage for each child.
- **POTENTIAL SIDE EFFECTS:** While melatonin is generally considered safe, it may have side effects including drowsiness, headaches and stomach issues. Long-term effects of melatonin use in children are not yet fully understood.
- **NOT A SUBSTITUTE FOR GOOD SLEEP HABITS:** Melatonin should not be used as a replacement for healthy sleep practices. Encouraging a consistent bedtime routine,

a calming sleep environment and limiting screen time before bed is crucial for good sleep hygiene in children, as we discussed in detail in chapter 6.
– **UNDERLYING CONDITIONS:** Melatonin may not be appropriate for all children, especially those with certain medical conditions or who are taking other medications. It is essential to consult a healthcare professional before giving melatonin to a child with any pre-existing health issues.

Medications for anxiety related to ADHD

Quite often, ADHD and anxiety exist together. If your child has been diagnosed with ADHD, they may be prescribed stimulants.

Fast-acting stimulants include Methylphenidate (Ritalin) and Dexamfetamine.

Most paediatricians will start with a fast-acting option to figure out the best dose and ensure there are no major side effects, before switching over to longer-acting stimulants which can last through the day. Examples include Methylphenidate hydrochloride (brand name Ritalin LA and Concerta) and Lisdexamfetamine (brand name Vyvanse).

While they are called 'stimulants', these medications can have a calming effect on a child's anxiety when it is related to ADHD. A broad, holistic view of your child's diagnosis is important as they undergo assessment and treatment.

Non-stimulant medications

Medications called alpha agonists were originally developed to lower blood pressure in adults. However, they were also found to reduce symptoms of anxiety by acting on the sympathetic nervous system, which regulates the body's fight-or-flight response. They can reduce the sensitivity of the body's alarm system so it does not go off as frequently or as intensely.

The alpha agonists prescribed for anxiety in children and teens include Catapres (clonidine) and Intuniv (guanfacine). Another non-stimulant is called Atomoxetine (Strattera). Strattera is a noradrenaline reuptake inhibitor and works in a similar way to the serotonin reuptake inhibitors that I have previously described. Generally speaking stimulant medications are first-line treatments for ADHD and non-stimulants are reserved for those who don't respond or cannot take stimulants due to side effects.

Mood-stabilising medications

Antipsychotics, a class of drugs initially developed to alleviate the symptoms of psychosis such as delusions and hallucinations in individuals with schizophrenia and bipolar disorder, are sometimes prescribed to children and adolescents dealing with severe, persistent anxiety. The following antipsychotics are the most commonly prescribed to children and teenagers with anxiety disorders: Risperdal (risperidone), Abilify (aripiprazole) and Seroquel (quetiapine).

For children with OCD, antipsychotics can be paired with antidepressants to curb obsessive thoughts. They can be effective for reducing rigidity and helping children with OCD who are plagued with extreme and unrealistic worries and thoughts.

It's important to use antipsychotics with caution as they can have detrimental side effects such as weight gain and metabolic, neurological and hormonal changes. Side effects also increase as the dose is increased. Generally, these medications are prescribed by a paediatrician or psychiatrist with experience and training in paediatric mental health.

CHAPTER 11

Case Studies

This chapter presents some more real-life examples of how anxiety can present in different ages.

CASE ONE

Coping with frequent crying

Sarah is a caring and devoted mother to an 18-month-old baby girl named Emma. Emma is otherwise healthy but has been displaying frequent crying episodes that are becoming overwhelming for both Sarah and the baby.

Frequent crying and emotional strain

Emma's frequent crying has become a constant source of worry and stress for Sarah. No matter what Sarah tries, Emma seems to be inconsolable at times, leading Sarah to feel helpless and emotionally drained. As a result, Sarah finds herself becoming increasingly anxious and emotional, unsure of how to soothe her baby.

Long working hours for dad

Adding to the challenge, Sarah's husband, Tom, works long hours to support the family, leaving Sarah to care for Emma by herself for most of the day. With limited opportunities for breaks or time to recharge, Sarah feels the weight of the responsibility resting heavily on her shoulders.

Seeking medical guidance

Recognising that Emma's crying is persistent and affecting both her and the baby's wellbeing, Sarah decides to seek medical guidance. She schedules an appointment with Emma's GP to rule out any underlying health issues or discomfort that might be causing the distress.

Receiving support from the GP

During the visit, the GP thoroughly examines Emma and finds no signs of any physical health problems. However, the GP offers valuable guidance to Sarah about common developmental milestones and the challenges some babies face in expressing themselves. The GP also provides some resources on sleep and settling babies and a referral to a local parent support network.

Understanding the baby's needs

With the GP's support, Sarah gains a better understanding of Emma's developmental stage and the reasons behind her frequent crying. The GP explains that, at 18 months, toddlers experience rapid cognitive, emotional and physical growth, leading to increased frustration as they struggle to communicate effectively.

Exploring communication techniques

Sarah learns about various communication techniques that can help her better understand Emma's needs and feelings. These techniques include observing Emma's body language, facial expressions and vocalisations to identify the possible reasons behind her crying.

Establishing a routine

The GP advises Sarah to establish a consistent daily routine for Emma to provide a sense of security and predictability. Having a structured routine can help reduce both Emma's and Sarah's anxiety and provide opportunities for self-care during designated times. The GP suggests that Sarah sets up the nursery as a calming environment, and for the next week, she uses this room for all day and night sleeps, rather than having Emma attached to her.

Seeking family and community support

Sarah reaches out to her extended family members and close friends for emotional support and assistance. Tom also makes a conscious effort to spend quality time with Emma whenever he is at home, helping Sarah get some much-needed rest and respite.

Finding parenting resources

Sarah actively seeks out parenting resources, books and online forums where she can connect with other parents facing similar challenges. Engaging with a supportive community allows her to share experiences, exchange advice and gain new coping strategies.

Professional counselling

Acknowledging her own emotional strain, Sarah decides to seek professional counselling through a psychologist to work through her anxiety and emotions. Counselling sessions offer her a safe space to express her feelings, learn coping mechanisms and build resilience.

Self-care and time for relaxation

Incorporating self-care into her daily routine, Sarah makes time for relaxation, exercise and pursuing hobbies that bring her joy. Taking care of her emotional wellbeing enables her to be a more patient and present parent for Emma. She adapts some 'tag teaming' with her husband so that they each get a dedicated time on the weekend to escape and unwind. They join the local gym and develop an exercise routine they can use in this time. Then they create some family rituals, including spending time together and going out for a coffee or to the local park.

As Sarah seeks medical guidance, understands Emma's needs, gains emotional support and prioritises self-care, she gradually finds a balance in caring for her daughter. She finds a parent-baby yoga group and then also realises the same gym has a creche so that she can attend other classes.

With time, patience and a supportive network, Sarah navigates the challenges of early parenthood, fostering a stronger bond with her baby and overcoming the emotional strain. Sarah also has a check-up with her own GP and finds that she is iron deficient. She has an iron infusion which gives her some additional energy.

Even when we feel we are acting calmly despite anxiety, babies have a sixth sense! They can detect our muscle tension, our mood swings and our communication changing when we have strong feelings. This is not to say we need to hide our emotions. In fact, quite the opposite: we need to get the right help to allow processing of these emotions. Share the journey so you are not isolated or alone.

CASE TWO

Coping with anxiety and emotional dysregulation

Jake is a bright and energetic four-year-old boy who has been displaying signs of anxiety and emotional dysregulation at home. His parents, Annie and Beth, are struggling to understand and manage his behaviour, as he frequently lashes out, experiences 'mega tantrums' and shows difficulty in regulating his emotions.

Recognising the signs

Annie and Beth notice a pattern of behaviours in Jake, such as frequent meltdowns over seemingly minor issues, heightened emotional reactions and difficulty transitioning between activities. They realise that his behaviour may be indicative of underlying anxiety and emotional challenges.

Seeking professional assessment

Concerned about their son's wellbeing and recognising the need for expert guidance, Annie decides to seek a professional assessment. She schedules an appointment with their local child health nurse who then sends her to the local GP.

Diagnosis and understanding

After a thorough evaluation, including an examination of Jake's ears and throat and a check of his growth and development, the GP provides Annie with a diagnosis of anxiety and emotional dysregulation in Jake. He also notes that there is likely to be low iron in Jake as he is very selective with his food and refusing to eat any vegetables. The GP arranges an iron test which confirms this and starts a course of iron supplements.

The GP utilises a mental health treatment plan to refer Jake to a mental health OT.

This helps with gaining a better understanding of the factors contributing to his behaviour, including recently commencing kindergarten, sensitivity to environmental changes, sensory difficulties with textures in food, stressors, and difficulty expressing his feelings.

Implementing coping strategies

With guidance from the OT, Annie and Beth start implementing coping strategies to help Jake manage his anxiety and emotions. They introduce visual schedules and routines to provide predictability and structure, which can help reduce transition-related anxiety.

They reduce any pressure on introducing new foods and try to gently introduce foods over time, without any emotion attached. Even though they feel frustrated, they try not to show it when Jake refuses to wear certain clothes with tags or socks that are crinkled up.

Encouraging emotional expression

Annie and Beth encourage Jake to express his emotions through words, drawings and play. They create a safe and supportive environment where he feels comfortable talking about his feelings, helping him build emotional literacy and understanding.

Teaching relaxation techniques

To assist Jake in managing his emotional dysregulation, Annie and Beth teach him simple relaxation techniques such as deep breathing and mindfulness exercises. These techniques help him calm down during moments of heightened emotions. They start up a 5 minute wind-down routine before bed where they all listen to a meditation podcast, dimming the lights and lying on the floor.

Limiting triggers and overstimulation

Recognising that Jake is quite sensitive to overstimulation to screens or noise, Annie and Beth take measures to limit this where possible. They take Jake for a short, quiet walk just before or after dinner and ensure all screens are off before bed, including their phones. They recognised that Jake often ate dinner early and was hungry before bed. They implemented a snack before bed, such as warm milk and milo or a low-sugar homemade muffin. They also spoke about how tired they both were at night. They agreed to refrain from discussing significant issues or topics right before bed, as this only ever ended in arguments. They wrote things down that they needed to discuss the next day. This not only helped their anxiety and stress, but it also helped Jake's, as everyone seemed calmer.

They create a calming and quiet space where he can retreat

during overwhelming moments, helping him regain control over his emotions.

Positive reinforcement

Annie and Beth use positive reinforcement to acknowledge Jake's efforts in managing his emotions and making progress. They praise him when he expresses himself calmly and appropriately, reinforcing positive behaviour. Jake also starts to take himself to his bedroom when he's worked up, learning how to spend time quietly winding down with some Lego before coming out to explain how he felt.

Seeking parenting support

To cope with the challenges of parenting a child with anxiety and emotional dysregulation, Annie and Beth attend parenting workshops including the Circle of Security. Learning from others in similar situations helps them exchange experiences and gain valuable insights.

They decide to seek individual counselling and parenting coaching to develop effective strategies for supporting Jake and managing their stress as parents. This counselling offers them tools to cope with challenging situations and nurture a positive family dynamic. They start listening to some parenting podcasts and reading relevant books.

Team approach

Annie and Beth involve teachers and caregivers in Jake's life to create a consistent and supportive environment. By sharing insights and strategies, they ensure everyone is working together to support his emotional wellbeing.

Celebrating progress

As Jake makes progress in managing his anxiety and emotions, his parents celebrate his achievements, no matter how small. They acknowledge the effort he puts into coping with difficult feelings and demonstrate their unwavering support and love.

Through a combination of professional guidance, coping strategies, a supportive environment and patience, they find ways to manage Jake's anxiety and emotional dysregulation. As they work together as a team, they help their four-year-old son navigate his emotions and foster a loving and nurturing environment for his growth and development.

Time also helps this situation to improve. Being four is a tricky age of brain development and learning self-expression. As clichéd as it sounds, this phase will pass even if treatment is not working as well as his parents had hoped. Keep your GP in the loop if you feel the behaviours are escalating, as four can be one of the ages that other conditions such as autism or ADHD may start to show symptoms. A paediatrician referral may also be required. Each of these practical steps also takes time, be kind to yourself and don't feel you need to rush this process or that it will all get better overnight. It won't. But remain hopeful of some happier times and improved bonding with your child despite the difficult emotions.

Also remember that children at this age are susceptible to medical causes of anxiety. There have been so many occasions where a child who might be head banging and irritable was later found to have an ear effusion (fluid behind the ear drum) or chronic ear infection. Or, as was the case with Jake, an underlying nutritional deficiency. This is where the holistic approach and consideration for the whole child can become important. You know your child best and if you feel there are other secondary causes at play, make sure these are reviewed. Refer back to the checklist in chapter 7.

CASE THREE

Separation anxiety after divorce

Min-Jun is an eight-year-old girl who has been struggling with separation anxiety when it comes to being dropped off at school. Her parents, Sun and Jae, are divorced but are committed to providing the best possible support for Min-Jun during this challenging time.

Min-Jun seems to be really anxious that her mum is going to die and she will be left alone or with just her dad to look after her. This is a common thought or feeling for an eight-year-old child and can be a trigger for other emotions or nightmares.

Acknowledging the impact of divorce

Sun and Jae understand that their divorce was a significant life change for Min-Jun, and they recognise the importance of addressing her separation anxiety with sensitivity and compassion. They have come to realise, through talking to Min-Jun, that when she is left with one parent she feels an overwhelming fear of losing the other parent and never seeing them again.

Effective communication

Despite their separation, Sun and Jae maintain open and effective communication about Min-Jun's wellbeing. They discuss her struggles with separation anxiety and work together to devise a consistent plan to help her cope.

Unified approach

Sun and Jae present a united front when addressing Min-Jun's anxiety. They assure her that both of them are there to support her and that she can always reach out to either parent for comfort and guidance. This takes place despite them not agreeing on all aspects of the plan. For example, Jae puts Min-Jun to bed about an hour later so that he gets more time with her at night as he only sees Min-Jun every second weekend. Sun disagrees on this, but they learn to accept they cannot do things perfectly in alignment.

Shared routines

Sun and Jae aim to establish similar routines at both of their homes to create a sense of continuity for Min-Jun. Having consistent morning rituals and school drop-off routines helps alleviate her anxiety.

Transition support

During transitions between homes, Sun and Jae prioritise Min-Jun's emotional needs. They allow her to bring comfort items or engage in calming activities during these times to provide reassurance.

School collaboration

Sun and Jae collaborate with Min-Jun's school and her teacher to keep them informed about her anxiety and home situation. The school offers additional support and understanding to help her adjust during this challenging period.

Gradual exposure

Both Sun and Jae work together to gradually expose Min-Jun to short periods of separation. They take turns dropping her off at school or engaging in planned activities to help her feel comfortable with the transition.

Family counselling

Recognising the impact of divorce on Min-Jun's emotions, Sun and Jae consider family counselling to navigate the challenges of separation anxiety together. A therapist can provide valuable guidance for co-parenting and supporting Min-Jun's emotional wellbeing.

Reinforcing positive experiences

Sun and Jae celebrate any progress Min-Jun makes in managing her anxiety, regardless of which parent she is with at the time. They offer praise and support for her efforts, emphasising that they are proud of her resilience.

Encouraging peer connections

Sun and Jae encourage Min-Jun to participate in extracurricular activities and playdates with her peers. Engaging in social interactions helps Min-Jun build friendships and create a sense of belonging.

Through effective co-parenting, shared routines and continuous communication, Sun and Jae provide the stability and understanding Min-Jun needs to cope with her separation anxiety. Their commitment to supporting her emotional wellbeing ensures that she feels loved, secure and better equipped to navigate school and daily challenges despite their divorce.

CASE FOUR

Online bullying

Emily is a bright and creative 13-year-old who loves expressing herself through art and writing. She is active on social media platforms, sharing her artwork and connecting with like-minded people. However, her positive online experience takes a dark turn when she becomes a victim of cyberbullying.

Incident and initial reaction

One day, Emily discovers hurtful and negative comments on her social media posts, attacking her art and personal interests. These cruel remarks are demoralising, and Emily starts feeling anxious every time she thinks about going online or posting something new. The fear of facing more hurtful comments and judgemental behaviour begins to impact her self-esteem and overall wellbeing.

Seeking support

At first, Emily tries to handle the situation on her own, but her anxiety continues to grow. Recognising the severity of the issue, she decides to confide in her parents and shares her experience of online bullying. They respond with empathy, understanding the emotional toll it's taking on her.

Encouraging open communication

Emily's parents assure her that she did nothing wrong and that online bullying is unacceptable. They create an environment of open communication, allowing Emily to freely express her feelings and concerns without judgement. They also encourage her to take breaks from social media to reduce the anxiety triggers.

Engaging school teachers

Emily's parents decide to involve her teacher, as the bullying originated from someone in her class. They also have a meeting with the school chaplain and principal to discuss the issue. The school takes the matter seriously and agrees to address the situation, emphasising the importance of respectful behaviour both online and offline.

Empowering coping strategies

While the school works on addressing the bullying, Emily's parents and counsellor help her develop coping strategies to manage her anxiety.

They introduce her to mindfulness exercises and deep breathing techniques to calm her mind during stressful moments. They also encourage her to engage in her hobbies, such as drawing and writing, as a way of expressing herself positively. In fact, it is her art that helps her to turn the anxiety around. Emily finds other ways to enjoy her art through painting murals at a local art club and selling artworks to raise money for a charity.

Building a support network

Emily's parents help her to identify supportive friends who share her interests and values. They encourage her to surround herself with positive influences and like-minded people online. Emily finds a friendly art community with people who appreciate her work and provide encouragement and constructive feedback.

Educating on online safety

Emily's parents teach her about privacy settings, the importance of not sharing personal information with strangers, and how to block and report cyberbullies. This knowledge gives Emily more confidence in navigating social media responsibly. They also thought it would be helpful to give Emily a break from using social media and being online. Despite Emily not being overly keen on the idea, her parents turn the wifi off from 7pm each night. This limits the opportunity for anyone in the house to use the wifi, and opens up more time for having family conversation and activities that help them unwind.

Seeking professional help

Despite the progress made, Emily's anxiety persists, especially when she goes to school. Her parents notice a pattern of tummy aches every Sunday night and on the mornings before school. Her parents decide to consult their GP for a check-up of the tummy pains and a mental health treatment plan. She is referred for some tests to rule out anything physical and onto a psychologist who specialises in adolescent anxiety and cyberbullying. Through therapy, Emily learns additional coping skills and gains insights into managing her emotions effectively.

Overcoming anxiety and moving forward

Over time, Emily's confidence grows, and she becomes more resilient. With the support of her family, school and mental health professionals, she learns to stand up against cyberbullying and not let negative comments define her self-worth. Emily continues to share her passion for art online, surrounding herself with positivity and constructive feedback. Her journey through anxiety related to online bullying has taught her valuable lessons about self-acceptance, the power of support and the importance of treating others with kindness both online and offline.

This example shows the time and patience it takes to work through anxiety but that it does get better. In saying that, Emily is vulnerable to experiencing this again. Bullies and cyberbullies are good at picking on those who are doing well or passionate about something. Emily will continue to develop her resilience so that on those tough days, she can find the right help and manage the feelings that arise out of difficult days.

CASE FIVE

Year 12 anxiety

Alex is a 17-year-old boy who is in his final year of school (Year 12). He has always been a diligent student, but as the pressure of exams intensifies, he begins to experience anxiety that negatively impacts his academic performance.

Increased anxiety and poor concentration

As the Year 12 exams draw near, Alex becomes increasingly anxious about his performance. He starts worrying excessively about not meeting his own expectations and the expectations of his parents and teachers. The fear of failure takes a toll on his ability to concentrate, making it difficult for him to focus on his studies.

Declining grades and heightened anxiety

Due to his poor concentration and increased anxiety, Alex's grades start to drop, further adding to his stress and self-doubt. The decline in academic performance reinforces his belief that he won't be able to cope with the pressure and expectations surrounding the exams.

Experimenting with marijuana

Feeling overwhelmed and seeking a way to alleviate his nerves, Alex decides to try marijuana. He believes it might help him relax and temporarily escape the pressures of exam preparation. He doesn't disclose this to his parents but when they do eventually take him to the GP, he mentions it when the GP sees him alone. The GP is understanding about what Alex is going through and gives him some education on why he might be using marijuana to treat his anxiety and also the harms this could lead to in the longer term. He makes some suggestions such as cutting back, stopping and looking at alternative ways to unwind. The GP assures Alex of confidentiality when they are speaking without his parents. The only time confidentiality can be broken is if Alex is at risk of immediate harm such as expressing suicidal ideations, self-harm or harm to someone else.

Recognising the problem and seeking help

As the situation escalates, Alex becomes aware that his approach is not healthy nor productive. He realises that using marijuana is not a sustainable solution and may even be exacerbating his anxiety and academic challenges. He starts to panic more that his parents will find out what he is doing, and the impact this will have. Teenagers will make mistakes. This is part of their impulsive brain and normal for their development. How they overcome these mistakes, and the support they receive from others, will be what builds their resilience and help their personal growth.

Supportive network

Alex confides in a close friend who listens empathetically and encourages him to talk to his parents about what he's going through. With the support of his friend, Alex finds the courage to approach his parents and share his feelings of anxiety and the impact on his studies.

Seeking professional guidance

Recognising the seriousness of the situation, Alex's parents decide to take him back to the GP for further discussion. They talk to Alex about ceasing his drug use, and he commences SSRI medication to help his anxiety. Since this medication can take at least six weeks to work, in the meantime, Alex does his best to develop other, more positive coping mechanisms.

Developing healthy coping mechanisms

Through therapy sessions with a psychologist, Alex learns various coping mechanisms to manage his exam-related anxiety. He practises mindfulness exercises, deep breathing techniques and time-management strategies to reduce stress and improve concentration.

Alex also joins the gym with a friend. He goes most days after school and pushes weights, which seems to help him feel happier and less overwhelmed. He also notices afterwards that he has more energy to study and is more focused.

Setting realistic goals

Alex's psychologist helps him set realistic and achievable goals for his exams. They focus on encouraging his personal growth and progress rather than solely aiming for perfect grades. This approach relieves some of the pressure and allows Alex to regain his confidence.

Building a study routine

With support from his parents and psychologist, Alex establishes a structured study routine that includes regular breaks and time for relaxation. This helps him stay organised and maintain a healthy balance.

Connecting with peers

Alex joins a study group with supportive peers who are also preparing for exams. This creates a sense of camaraderie and allows him to share study tips and emotional support with others facing similar challenges.

Positive reinforcement

Alex's parents provide positive reinforcement and encouragement throughout his exam preparation journey. They celebrate his efforts, progress and commitment to overcoming his anxiety.

Achieving success through resilience

As Alex puts these coping mechanisms into practice, he begins to see a positive change in his attitude and academic performance. He starts to feel less stressed once the SSRI has reached the right dose. His improved focus and emotional wellbeing lead to better exam results, reinforcing his belief in his ability to cope with challenging situations.

By addressing his anxiety, seeking professional help and adopting healthier coping strategies, Alex not only achieves better academic outcomes but also gains valuable life skills to manage stress and anxiety in the future.

CASE SIX

Anxiety, self-harm and substance use

Laura is a 16-year-old teenager going through a tumultuous phase marked by anxiety, self-harm thoughts, school refusal and substance use. Laura's single mother, Simone, is deeply concerned about their wellbeing and seeks help to address these challenging issues.

Identifying the struggles

Simone notices a significant change in Laura's behaviour. She has become increasingly withdrawn and irritable, and expresses feelings of hopelessness. Simone becomes aware of the self-harm thoughts and discovers that Laura has been skipping school and engaging in substance use.

Reaching out for support

Simone takes the initiative to seek professional help. She schedules an appointment with their family GP to assess Laura's mental and emotional wellbeing.

Introducing antidepressant medication

Based on the assessment, the GP prescribes an SSRI (fluoxetine) to help alleviate Laura's symptoms of anxiety and depression. Simone ensures that Laura understands the importance of adhering to the prescribed treatment plan and attends regular follow-up appointments with her GP. This takes some convincing as Laura doesn't want to 'take a pill' for her problems. The GP explained that this is only one small part of the treatment plan that will give her the confidence to cope with what she is facing. He reassures Laura the medication won't change who she is or her personality. Laura is still reluctant about this idea. Her GP was very understanding and further explained that she will feel so much better and no longer be overwhelmed, but to do this she needs to commit to the treatment and work hard at climbing back up the mountain.

Supporting sleep with melatonin

Given Laura's sleep difficulties, the GP also recommends melatonin to regulate her sleep patterns. Simone introduces melatonin along with a better bedtime routine to improve Laura's sleep quality.

Referral to child and adolescent health service

The GP refers Laura to Headspace using a mental health care plan to provide comprehensive support. Headspace is a local, government-funded counselling service for teenagers aged 12 to 25.

It took around eight weeks to start this therapy due to the waiting time to access it. In advance, Laura began looking at their website which is called eHeadspace online, where she found some valuable resources. Before she went to the counsellor, she wrote down some goals in a journal: 'To stop feeling so anxious', 'To start something that makes me happy', and 'To know how to stop cutting myself'. On seeing her counsellor, she started working with them to address the underlying causes of anxiety, self-harm thoughts and substance use. The GP also refers Laura to a private adolescent psychiatrist. However, the wait time will be many months for the first appointment. Her Mum found she had to call several clinics to find someone to accept the referral.

Challenges and setbacks

As Laura begins her journey towards healing, she encounters ups and downs. Some days are better than others, and recovery is not always smooth. Hormones also challenge Laura, and she notices a big jump in anxiety just before her period starts. During this time, Simone finds Laura very difficult to manage. The GP monitors things with fortnightly appointments and sees Laura on her own to check in on her self-harming. Laura tells the GP she thinks a lot about cutting but has managed to distract herself with fidgets, using her phone and chatting to friends. The GP suggests increasing the dose of the SSRI to help support her emotions around her period. He describes a condition called 'Premenstrual Dysphoric Disorder' (PMDD), which leads to extreme emotions, either anxiety or depression or a mix of both, around the time of her period. It can also lead to worsening self-harm thoughts. The GP asks Laura to track her period so she can be aware of when she will experience worsening symptoms. Together, they create a safety plan so she can refer to this if she isn't coping.

Promoting a supportive environment

Simone encourages open communication and creates a supportive environment at home for Laura to express her feelings without judgement. She involves Laura in decision-making about her treatment and encourages her to engage in hobbies and activities she once enjoyed. They head out on weekends for bush walks, and have spontaneous coffee dates together.

Simone prints a picture she made that lists all Laura's nice attributes, such as being generous, kind, funny, and creative. She decorates the picture for Laura's wall so that they can be reminded of all the good things in her life.

Coping strategies and self-care

Through counselling, Laura learns healthy coping strategies to manage her anxiety and self-harm thoughts constructively. The counsellor emphasises self-care practices, such as mindfulness, art therapy and physical activities, to help Laura build resilience and manage stress.

Community support

Simone seeks out community support groups for Laura and herself to connect with others who have faced similar challenges. She finds a local church group that meets once a week and a book club where they talk about a 'book of the month'. The support group offers empathy, understanding, and a sense of belonging, helping them realise they are not alone in their journey.

Long-term commitment

Despite the rocky road ahead, Simone's unwavering love and proactive approach to seeking professional help significantly impact Sofia's wellbeing. She remains dedicated to supporting Sofia's mental health and provides unconditional love and reassurance during the recovery process. Even when Simone enters into a new relationship with Brad, she maintains her time for Sofia so that she remains the key focus in her life. This isn't always easy and Simone is aware that she doesn't need to be perfect but just try her best to support Sofia. With a combination of medication, therapy, community support and family understanding, Sofia begins to find their path towards healing and recovery, building hope for a brighter future.

Conclusion

Just from reading this book you have shown an interest in supporting your child or someone you know who might be troubled by anxiety.

We are experiencing a strong rise in anxiety across the world right now, which can only mean we all need to slow down and become more present. Learning to be present – accepting that the past is the past and already completed, and the future is unwritten and unable to be controlled – is one of the most important skills in developing a calmer state of mind.

Teaching our children this will help them to cope better when faced with stress. Modelling appropriate reactions in front of our children, and reflecting with them when we, too, might make a mistake, are key parenting skills in building happier households.

Finally, we must learn to have fun with our kids, avoid judging them or overreacting, and be fair with them so they feel valued and know they have adults they can turn to when difficulties are overwhelming.

Resources

Throughout this book I've mentioned a number of resources that I have collected over the years I have been treating and managing children with anxiety. I've listed these below for your reference. While not all resources may be evidence-based or scientifically backed, they are simple and easy to understand and provide some very useful strategies for you and your family.

Books for children aged three to seven

Hey Warrior series by Karen Young
Worries are Not Forever by Elizabeth Verdick and Marieka Heinlen
The Don't Worry Book by Todd Parr
Too Many Bubbles: A Story about Mindfulness by Christine Peck and Mags DeRoma
Ruby Finds a Worry by Tom Percival

Books for children aged four to eight

Ish by Peter A Reynolds
The Dot by Peter A Reynolds

Beautiful Oops by Barney Saltzberg
The Whatifs by Emily Kilgore and Zoe Persico
Hey Warrior: a book for kids about anxiety by Karen Young
Brave Every Day by Trudy Ludwig and Patrice Barton
Black Dog by Levi Pinfold
Fraidyzoo by Thyra Heder
When Worry Takes Hold by Liz Haske and InSong Nam
Me and My Fear by Francesca Sanna
Wilma Jean the Worry Machine by Julia Cook and Anita DuFalla
The Kissing Hand by Audrey Penn
Chester the Brave by Audrey Penn
Don't Think About Purple Elephants by Susan Whelan
Llama Llama Misses Mama by Anna Dewdney

Books for children aged six to 12

What to do When the News Scares You by Jacqueline B Toner and Janet McDonnell
The Worry Workbook for Kids by Muniya Khanna and Deborah Roth Ledley
The Self-Regulation Workbook for Kids by Jenna Berman
The Relaxation and Stress Reduction Workbook for Kids by Lawrence Shapiro and Robin Sprague
Growing Pangs by Kathryn Ormsbee and Molly Brooks
Better with Butter by Victoria Piontek
The Invisible String by Patrice Karst

Books for children age nine to 14

Guts by Raina Telgemeier
Outsmarting Worry: An Older Kid's Guide to Managing Anxiety by Dawn Huebner

The Deepest Breath by Meg Grehan
The Summer of June by Jamie Sumner
The Unforgettable What's his Name by Paul Jennings

Books for teenagers

The Teen Girl's Anxiety Survival Guide: 10 Ways to Conquer Anxiety and Feel Your Best by Lucie Hemmen
Anxiety Sucks! A Teen Survival Guide by Natasha Daniels
The Anxiety Workbook for Teens by Lisa Schab
Rewire your Anxious Brain for Teens by Debra Kissen, Ashley Kendall, Michelle Lozano and Micah Ioffe
The Perfectionism Workbook for Teens by Ann Marie Dobosz
Mindfulness for Teen Worry by Jeffrey Bernstein
The Panic Workbook for Teens by Debra Kissen, Bari Goldman Cohen and Kathi Fine Abitbol
The Mindful Breathing Workbook for Teens by Matthew Dewar
The Shyness and Social Anxiety Workbook for Teens by Jennifer Shannon

Gratitude journals for children

The 3 Minute Gratitude Journal for Kids: A Journal to Teach Children to Practice Gratitude and Mindfulness by Modern Kid Press
Daily Gratitude Journal for Kids: https://calmstore.com.au/product/kids-daily-gratitude-journal

Books for adults

Anxious Kids by Michael Grose and Jodi Richardson
Brain-Body Parenting: How to Stop Managing Behaviour and Start Raising Joyful, Resilient Kids by Mona Delahooke

Raising Girls Who Like Themselves by Kasey Edwards and Dr Christopher Scanlan

Bringing up Boys Who Like Themselves by Kasey Edwards and Dr Christopher Scanlan

No Drama Discipline: The Whole-Brain Way to Calm the Chaos and Nurture Your Child's Developing Mind by Tina Bryson and Daniel Siegel

The Yes Brain Child: Help Your Child be More Resilient, Independent and Creative by Tina Bryson and Daniel Siegel

The Parenting Revolution: A Guide to Raising Resilient Kids by Justin Coulson

9 Ways to a Resilient Child by Justin Coulson

Helping your Anxious Child: A Step-by-Step Guide for Parents by Ronald M Rapee, Ann Wignall, Susan H Spence, Heidi Lyneham and Vanessa Cobham

Worry-Proofing your Anxious Child by Bev Aisbett

The Opposite of Worry: The Playoff Parenting Approach to Childhood Anxieties and Fears by Lawrence Cohen

Anxiety Relief for Kids: On-the-Spot Strategies to Help your Child Overcome Worry, Panic and Avoidance by Bridget Walker

Freeing your Child from Anxiety by Tamar Chansky

The Whole-Brain Child: 12 Revolutionary Strategies to Nurture your Child's Developing Mind by Daniel Siegel and Tina Bryson

When the World Feels Like a Scary Place: Essential Conversations for Anxious Parents and Worried Kids by Abigail Gewirtz

The Book you Wish Your Parents Had Read (and your Children will be Glad that you Did) by Philippa Perry

The Explosive Child: A New Approach for Understanding and Parenting Easily Frustrated, Chronically Inflexible Children by Ross Greene

The Resilience Project: Finding Happiness through Gratitude Empathy & Mindfulness by Hugh Van Cuylenburg

Apps

Smiling Mind
- Each age group can work their way through a series of different exercises. For example, there are eight exercises for seven to 11-year-olds, and 10 exercises for 12 to 15-year-olds.
- Each exercise works on a different aspect of mindfulness, such as breathing, exploring taste or exploring sound. There is no need to work through the exercises in a particular order.
- It is Australian and has a calming Australian voice that can be less distracting for Aussie kids than other programs with different accents.
- It is free!

Headspace
- This meditation app can be used by the whole family.
- Meditation has been shown to help people stress less, focus more and even sleep better. Headspace is meditation made simple. They'll teach you the life-changing skills of meditation and mindfulness in just a few minutes a day.
- An annual subscription is around $90 to $100.

ConversationBuilder
- There are lots of options to choose from in this app to support conversation and social skills.
- The child can select conversations in which they are the initiator or conversations in which a peer is the initiator. They can also select how many exchanges will occur

in the conversation. For example, four exchanges in a conversation would mean that the child says something, the other person responds, the child says something back and then the other person responds again.
- The program gives them feedback about their choice. For example, the program will explain if the child chooses to say a statement where a question is more appropriate.
- The child can record the sentence they have chosen as a response. They can press the record button after each exchange and then listen to what the other person says in response. In the end, they can listen to the whole conversation from start to finish.
- Kids love it!

My DPS (Digital Problem Solver)
- A very easy-to-use app with minimal language requirements that helps children identify their emotions.
- Once the child has selected how they are feeling, there are several strategies suggested to help them cope. For example, 'Take a Break to Calm Down' or 'Take Five Deep Breaths'.
- You can add your own coping strategies.
- Children are encouraged to take photos of themselves coping in different ways and build up a bank of problem-solving techniques.
- The app also includes positive emotions and congratulates children for being happy!
- It costs less than $1.

Breathe, Think, Do with Sesame
- Laugh and learn as you help a *Sesame Street* monster friend calm down and solve everyday challenges.
- This bilingual (English and Spanish), research-based app helps your child learn Sesame's 'Breathe, Think, Do' strategy for problem-solving.
- Tap and touch to help the monster friend take deep breaths, think of plans and try them out. Your child will enjoy silly animations and playful interactions as they are exposed to important emotional vocabulary, a calm breathing technique, personalised encouragements and more!

Websites

Worry Wise Kids
worrywisekids.org

Provides parents, educators and mental health professionals with comprehensive, user-friendly information on the full range of anxiety disorders: how to identify symptoms, find effective treatments and prevent anxiety from taking hold in a child's life.

Brave
brave4you.psy.uq.edu.au

Brave is a free online treatment program based on CBT and designed for young people aged eight to 17 who are experiencing anxiety. There is also a supporting program for the young person's parents.

There are two separate programs; one for children aged eight to 12 years, and another for teenagers aged 12 to 17 years.

The program features:
- An audio track with guided exercises for deep breathing,

muscle relaxation, guided imagery and other anxiety-reduction techniques.
- An interactive Brave Ladder: a tool for planning and managing stepped exposure to sources of anxiety.

The program is free but the user is required to register before commencement and it's only available within Australia.

Raising Children Network
raisingchildren.net.au

Raising Children Network is an Australian Government-funded website that provides evidence-based tips and tools for everyday parenting from pregnancy to teens. It is a free resource viewed over 50,000 times per day. I recommend searching the site for 'strategies to support children with anxiety and fears'.

Beyond Blue
beyondblue.org.au

Beyond Blue offers parenting information and resources to support mental health and wellbeing for children, young people and families. Search for 'strategies to support anxious children'.

Cool Little Kids
coollittlekids.org.au

Cool Little Kids is an online program for Australian parents of shy or anxious young children aged three to six years.

Kids Helpline
kidshelpline.com.au

Young people can use kids helpline about all kinds of things including friendships and relationships, family issues, bullying and cyberbullying, school and study stress, gender identity, sexuality, mental health, feeling sad or upset, body issues, or because they're feeling unsafe.

The Circle of Security

circleofsecurityinternational.com

The Circle of Security is a parent/child psychotherapy program designed to assist parents to provide their children with the emotional support needed to develop secure attachment, resilience and enhanced school readiness.

Triple p parenting program

www.triplep-parenting.net.au

The Triple P – Positive Parenting Program is one of the most effective evidence-based parenting programs in the world, backed up by more than 35 years of ongoing research. Triple P gives parents simple and practical strategies to help them build strong, healthy relationships, confidently manage their children's behaviour and prevent problems developing. Triple P is used in more 30 countries and has been shown to work across cultures, socio-economic groups and in many different kinds of family structures.

Bringing up Great Kids (BUGK)

professionals.childhood.org.au/bringing-up-great-kids

Developed and established by Australian Childhood Foundation in 2005, Bringing Up Great Kids (BUGK) is a long-running and acclaimed program with more than 4000 registered facilitators trained nationally. It has had more than 50,000 parents benefit from it since it started.

The BUGK program is an integrated suite of unique activities and tools that offer all parents and carers a fresh way to understand and enact relationships with their children.

It has been evaluated and found to be an effective program in supporting the development of mindful and positive relationships between parents/carers and children.

It focuses on building positive and nurturing relationships between parents and their children. The program aims to support parents in reviewing and enhancing their patterns of communication with their children, promoting more respectful interactions, and encouraging the development of children's positive self-identity.

Podcasts

The Kids Health Network with Dr Andrew Leech

Of course, I will first mention my podcast series! It includes various episodes about anxiety, emotional regulation, and related conditions, as well as interviews with specialists and health professionals such as psychologists and occupational therapists.

The Emerging Minds podcast

https://emergingminds.com.au/resources/podcast/responding-to-child-anxiety-in-general-practice

During this episode of the *Emerging Minds* podcast, I discussed the impact of the Covid-19 pandemic on child anxiety, anxiety presentations by age and stage, strategies to support children experiencing anxiety, and how to recognise when further specialist support might be needed. Emerging Minds has other podcast episodes about mental health in children which are also useful for parents to listen to.

Parental as Anything with Maggie Dent

Maggie Dent has become one of Australia's favourite parenting authors and educators, with a particular interest in the early years, adolescence and resilience.

Happy Families

The *Happy Families* podcast with Dr Justin Coulson is designed for the time-poor parent who just wants answers now. Justin and his wife Kylie provide practical tips and a commonsense approach to parenting that families all over the world are connecting with.

Dr Golly and the Experts Podcast

We all start parenting as beginners, but imagine the learning curve when things don't go to plan. Dr Golly delves into the hard-earned wisdom of parents who have faced tough times and emerged as Experts.

Dr Golly is a paediatrician and invites parents to share their experiences.

Acknowledgements

Writing *Calm Kids, Happy Hearts* has been an incredible journey, and I am deeply grateful to those who have supported me along the way. First and foremost, I want to thank my family: my wife, Tanya, and our daughters, Charlotte and Isabelle. Your patience, love, and encouragement have been unwavering and essential every step of the way.

I am also immensely grateful to my parents, Patrick and Teresa. As an only child, your support has been the foundation of all my achievements. To Tanya's parents, Kim and Kaye, your support and kindness have been invaluable to our family, and I am deeply thankful.

A heartfelt thank you to the entire team at the Garden Family Medical Clinic. You truly are 'the dream team'. Each member brings unique strengths and dedicates themselves fully to our mission of supporting children and their families. Your commitment and passion are the heart of our success.

I also want to extend my deepest gratitude to the children and families I see in my practice as a GP. Thank you for allowing me the privilege to be a part of your lives and to help you towards better mental health. Your trust and openness inspire me every day.

I also extend my gratitude to the organisations that have provided me with the platform to advocate, educate and learn about childhood anxiety. Their resources and support have been instrumental in shaping this book. Special thanks to:

- The RACGP (www.racgp.org.au)
- Emerging Minds (https://emergingminds.com.au)
- Mental Health Professionals Network (www.mhpn.org.au)
- ADHD WA (www.adhdwa.org)

Thank you all for your continued support and dedication to improving the lives of children and their families.

About the Author

Dr Andrew Leech is an award-winning general practitioner (GP) and Director and Founder of the Garden Family Medical Clinic, a multidisciplinary, innovative GP clinic located in both Murdoch and Piara Waters in the south of Perth. He is a proud father of two children, Charlotte and Isabelle, and husband to his wife Tanya who works with him as a registered nurse.

Andrew has been a GP for 10 years. He has obtained additional training in child health through formal study at the University of Sydney, and via continuous collaboration with the many leading paediatricians, psychiatrists, allied health professionals and families he sees.

In 2023 he was honoured to be named the Royal Australian College of General Practitioners (RACGP) GP of the Year in Western Australia for his efforts in campaigning and advocating for child and adolescent mental health. Garden Family Medical Clinic was also nominated for the Australian Small Business of the Year award in 2023 and 2024.

Andrew firmly believes that children's mental health is crucial to their overall wellbeing and that it should be a top priority for families, schools, governments and the healthcare sector. He sees a wide range of paediatric mental health problems. Anxiety is currently the most common presenting problem across all age groups in primary healthcare.

Andrew is a key GP advisor on child development services in Western Australia and has represented general practice at a state and federal level at parliamentary enquiries into improving ADHD and mental health treatment access. He recently advised the Parliament of Western Australia's enquiry into child development services, and its report incorporated information gleaned from Andrew's presentation.[25]

Andrew is an active committee member and advisor for several organisations including the RACGP, ADHD WA, Emerging Minds, the Mental Health Professionals' Network (MHPN), the Australian Medical Association (AMA), Curtin University, the University of Notre Dame, ThinkGP, newsGP, Australian Doctor and Healthed.

He is a regular media contributor on the topic of child and adolescent health, including for the ABC, *The West Australian*, *PerthNow*, Channel 7, Channel 10 and 6PR radio.

He also works for Emerging Minds as a key advisor, developing resources for healthcare professionals and educators to assist them in supporting mental health in young people.

Andrew was the only GP representative on the Clinical Expert Advisory Group (EAG), supporting the Ministerial Taskforce into Public Mental Health Services for Infants, Children and Adolescents aged zero to 18 years in Western Australia.

Andrew has worked for Headspace and gained unique insights into young people's lives through this experience. He trains future doctors at the Notre Dame Medical School where he is an Adjunct Senior Lecturer. He also teaches and supervises junior GPs and has held teaching roles at Curtin University and Edith Cowan University.

He is a contributor to ParentTV and has produced his own podcast series: *The Kids Health Network*.

Visit drandrewleech.com for links to Andrew's recent media appearances and other work.

Dr Andrew Leech at the Garden Family Medical Clinic, Murdoch.

References

1. Australian Institute of Health and Welfare, 'Australia's children', 2023. www.aihw.gov.au/reports/children-youth/australias-children/contents/about
2. Ibid.
3. RCH, National Child Health Poll, 2022. www.rchpoll.org.au/wp-content/uploads/2022/10/NCHP-Special-Poll-AnxietyReport-FA.pdf
4. Australian Bureau of Statistics, 'National Study of Mental Health and Wellbeing', 2023. www.abs.gov.au/statistics/health/mental-health/national-study-mental-health-and-wellbeing/latest-release
5. Michelle G Craske and Murray B Stein, 'Anxiety', *The Lancet*, 2016, 388(10063).
6. Royal Children's Hospital Melbourne, 'Anxiety - primary school aged children', 2022. www.rch.org.au/kidsinfo/anxiety
7. Centers for Disease Control and Prevention (CDC), 'About the CDC-Kaiser ACE Study', 2021. www.cdc.gov/violenceprevention/aces/about.html
8. National Mental Health Commission, *Monitoring mental health and suicide prevention reform – National Report 2019*, 2019. www.mentalhealthcommission.gov.au/sites/default/files/2024-03/national-report-2019---summary.pdf
9. Young Minds Matter, 2013–2014. https://youngmindsmatter.telethonkids.org.au.
10. Australian Institute of Health and Welfare, op. cit.
11. Ibid.
12. Bitsko RH et al., 'Surveillance of Children's Mental Health – United States, 2013 – 2019', *MMWR*, 2022, 71:1–42.
13. Raising Children Network, 'Generalised anxiety in children', 2023. https://raisingchildren.net.au/toddlers/health-daily-care/mental-health/generalised-anxiety

14 Young Minds Matter, op. cit.
15 Claire Advokat and Mindy Scheithauer, 'Attention-deficit hyperactivity disorder (ADHD) stimulant medications as cognitive enhancers', *Front Neurosci.*, 2013; 7: 82.
16 Sudheer Kumar Muppalla et al., 'Effects of Excessive Screen Time on Child Development: An Updated Review and Strategies for Management', *Cureus.*, 2023, 15(6).
17 Australian Institute of Health and Welfare, 'Australia's children', 2023. https://www.aihw.gov.au/reports/children-youth/australias-children/contents/health/children-mental-illness
18 Circle of Security International, 'What is The Circle of Security?', 2022. www.circleofsecurityinternational.com/circle-of-security-model/what-is-the-circle-of-security/
19 Daily Telegraph, 'Mothers asked nearly 300 questions a day, study finds', 2013. www.telegraph.co.uk/news/uknews/9959026/Mothers-asked-nearly-300-questions-a-day-study-finds.html
20 Amy Fleming, 'Changing tastes: food and ageing', *The Guardian*, 2013. www.theguardian.com/lifeandstyle/wordofmouth/2013/jan/29/changing-tastes-food-and-aging
21 Ellyn Satter Institute, 'Raise a healthy child who is a joy to feed', 2024. www.ellynsatterinstitute.org/how-to-feed/the-division-of-responsibility-in-feeding/
22 Dietitian Connection, 'Fussy Eaters Factsheet', 2021. https://dietitianconnection.com/app/uploads/2021/06/Fussy-Eaters-Factsheet_A4-v6-1.pdf
23 Centre for Digital Wellbeing, *The Impacts of Social Media in Australia*, 2021. https://digitalwellbeing.org.au/wp-content/uploads/2021/12/Research-Brief-Impacts-of-Social-Media-in-Australia.pdf
24 Queensland Government, *Screen time and children*, 2015. https://earlychildhood.qld.gov.au/earlyYears/Documents/pts-screen-time-and-children.pdf
25 Parliament of Western Australia, *Child development services in Western Australia: Valuing our children and their needs*, 2024. https://www.parliament.wa.gov.au/Parliament/commit.nsf/(EvidenceOnly)/4F80772DF02D4AE6482588B0000A7782#Report

www.ingramcontent.com/pod-product-compliance
Lightning Source LLC
Chambersburg PA
CBHW071959290426
44109CB00018B/2077